Interactive Notebooks
LANGUAGE ARTS

Grade 1

Credits

Content Editor: Angela Triplett

Visit *carsondellosa.com* for correlations to Common Core, state, national, and Canadian provincial standards.

Carson-Dellosa Publishing, LLC
PO Box 35665
Greensboro, NC 27425 USA
carsondellosa.com

978-1-4838-2468-0
01-173157784

Table of Contents

© Carson-Dellosa • CD-104652

What Are Interactive Notebooks?

Interactive notebooks are a unique form of note taking. Teachers guide students through creating pages of notes on new topics. Instead of being in the traditional linear, handwritten format, notes are colorful and spread across the pages. Notes also often include drawings, diagrams, and 3-D elements to make the material understandable and relevant. Students are encouraged to complete their notebook pages in ways that make sense to them. With this personalization, no two pages are exactly the same.

Because of their creative nature, interactive notebooks allow students to be active participants in their own learning. Teachers can easily differentiate pages to address the levels and needs of each learner. The notebooks are arranged sequentially, and students can create tables of contents as they create pages, making it simple for students to use their notebooks for reference throughout the year. The interactive, easily personalized format makes interactive notebooks ideal for engaging students in learning new concepts.

Using interactive notebooks can take as much or as little time as you like. Students will initially take longer to create pages but will get faster as they become familiar with the process of creating pages. You may choose to only create a notebook page as a class at the beginning of each unit, or you may choose to create a new page for each topic within a unit. You can decide what works best for your students and schedule.

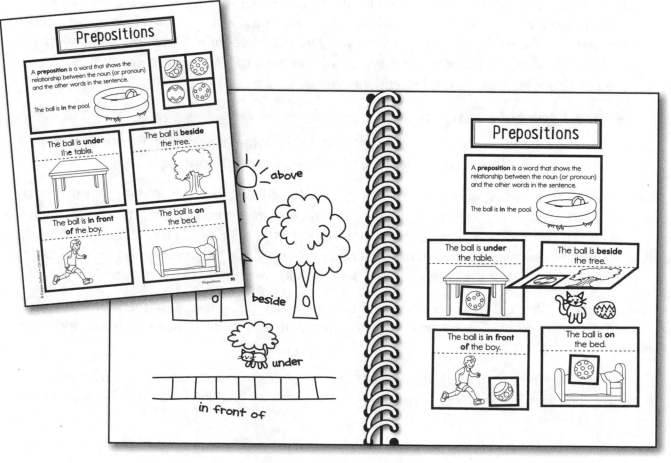

A student's interactive notebook for prepositions

Getting Started

You can start using interactive notebooks at any point in the school year. Use the following guidelines to help you get started in your classroom. (For more specific details, management ideas, and tips, see page 10.)

1. **Plan each notebook.**

   Use the planning template (page 9) to lay out a general plan for the topics you plan to cover in each notebook for the year.

2. **Choose a notebook type.**

   Interactive notebooks are usually either single-subject, spiral-bound notebooks; composition books; or three-ring binders with loose-leaf paper. Each type presents pros and cons. See page 5 for a more in-depth look at each type of notebook.

3. **Allow students to personalize their notebooks.**

   Have students decorate their notebook covers, as well as add their names and subjects. This provides a sense of ownership and emphasizes the personalized nature of the notebooks.

4. **Number the pages and create the table of contents.**

   Have students number the bottom outside corner of each page, front and back. When completing a new page, adding a table of contents entry will be easy. Have students title the first page of each notebook "Table of Contents." Have them leave several blank pages at the front of each notebook for the table of contents. Refer to your general plan for an idea of about how many entries students will be creating.

5. **Start creating pages.**

   Always begin a new page by adding an entry to the table of contents. Create the first notebook pages along with students to model proper format and expectations.

This book contains individual topics for you to introduce. Use the pages in the order that best fits your curriculum. You may also choose to alter the content presented to better match your school's curriculum. The provided lesson plans often do not instruct students to add color. Students should make their own choices about personalizing the content in ways that make sense to them. Encourage students to highlight and color the pages as they desire while creating them.

After introducing topics, you may choose to add more practice pages. Use the reproducibles (pages 78–96) to easily create new notebook pages for practice or to introduce topics not addressed in this book.

Use the grading rubric (page 11) to grade students' interactive notebooks at various points throughout the year. Provide students with copies of the rubric to glue into their notebooks and refer to as they create pages.

What Type of Notebook Should I Use?

Spiral Notebook

The pages in this book are formatted for a standard one-subject notebook.

Pros

- Notebook can be folded in half.
- Page size is larger.
- It is inexpensive.
- It often comes with pockets for storing materials.

Cons

- Pages can easily fall out.
- Spirals can snag or become misshapen.
- Page count and size vary widely.
- It is not as durable as a binder.

Tips

- Encase the spiral in duct tape to make it more durable.
- Keep the notebooks in a central place to prevent them from getting damaged in desks.

Composition Notebook

Pros

- Pages don't easily fall out.
- Page size and page count are standard.
- It is inexpensive.

Cons

- Notebook cannot be folded in half.
- Page size is smaller.
- It is not as durable as a binder.

Tips

- Copy pages meant for standard-sized notebooks at 85 or 90 percent. Test to see which works better for your notebook.

Binder with Loose-Leaf Paper

Pros

- Pages can be easily added, moved, or removed.
- Pages can be removed individually for grading.
- You can add full-page printed handouts.
- It has durable covers.

Cons

- Pages can easily fall out.
- Pages aren't durable.
- It is more expensive than a notebook.
- Students can easily misplace or lose pages.
- Larger size makes it more difficult to store.

Tips

- Provide hole reinforcers for damaged pages.

How to Organize an Interactive Notebook

You may organize an interactive notebook in many different ways. You may choose to organize it by unit and work sequentially through the book. Or, you may choose to create different sections that you will revisit and add to throughout the year. Choose the format that works best for your students and subject.

An interactive notebook includes different types of pages in addition to the pages students create. Non-content pages you may want to add include the following:

Title Page

This page is useful for quickly identifying notebooks. It is especially helpful in classrooms that use multiple interactive notebooks for different subjects. Have students write the subject (such as "Language Arts") on the title page of each interactive notebook. They should also include their full names. You may choose to have them include other information such as the teacher's name, classroom number, or class period.

Table of Contents

The table of contents is an integral part of the interactive notebook. It makes referencing previously created pages quick and easy for students. Make sure that students leave several pages at the beginning of each notebook for a table of contents.

Expectations and Grading Rubric

It is helpful for each student to have a copy of the expectations for creating interactive notebook pages. You may choose to include a list of expectations for parents and students to sign, as well as a grading rubric (page 11).

Unit Title Pages

Consider using a single page at the beginning of each section to separate it. Title the page with the unit name. Add a tab (page 78) to the edge of the page to make it easy to flip to the unit. Add a table of contents for only the pages in that unit.

Glossary

Reserve a six-page section at the back of the notebook where students can create a glossary. Draw a line to split in half the front and back of each page, creating 24 sections. Combine Q and R and Y and Z to fit the entire alphabet. Have students add an entry as each new vocabulary word is introduced.

Formatting Student Notebook Pages

The other major consideration for planning an interactive notebook is how to treat the left and right sides of a notebook spread. Interactive journals are usually viewed with the notebook open flat. This creates a left side and a right side. You have several options for how to treat the two sides of the spread.

Traditionally, the right side is used for the teacher-directed part of the lesson, and the left side is used for students to interact with the lesson content. The lessons in this book use this format. However, you may prefer to switch the order for your class so that the teacher-directed learning is on the left and the student input is on the right.

It can also be important to include standards, learning objectives, or essential questions in interactive notebooks. You may choose to write these on the top-left side of each page before completing the teacher-directed page on the right side. You may also choose to have students include the "Introduction" part of each lesson in that same top-left section. This is the *in, through, out* method. Students enter *in* the lesson on the top left of the page, go *through* the lesson on the right page, and exit *out* of the lesson on the bottom left with a reflection activity.

The following chart details different types of items and activities that you could include on each side.

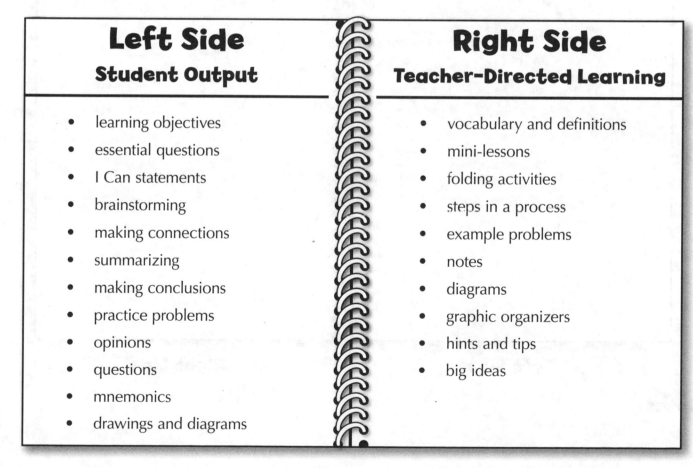

Left Side Student Output	Right Side Teacher-Directed Learning
• learning objectives	• vocabulary and definitions
• essential questions	• mini-lessons
• I Can statements	• folding activities
• brainstorming	• steps in a process
• making connections	• example problems
• summarizing	• notes
• making conclusions	• diagrams
• practice problems	• graphic organizers
• opinions	• hints and tips
• questions	• big ideas
• mnemonics	
• drawings and diagrams	

Planning for the Year

Making a general plan for interactive notebooks will help with planning, grading, and testing throughout the year. You do not need to plan every single page, but knowing what topics you will cover and in what order can be helpful in many ways.

Use the Interactive Notebook Plan (page 9) to plan your units and topics and where they should be placed in the notebooks. Remember to include enough pages at the beginning for the non-content pages, such as the title page, table of contents, and grading rubric. You may also want to leave a page at the beginning of each unit to place a mini table of contents for just that section.

In addition, when planning new pages, it can be helpful to sketch the pieces you will need to create. Use the following notebook template and notes to plan new pages.

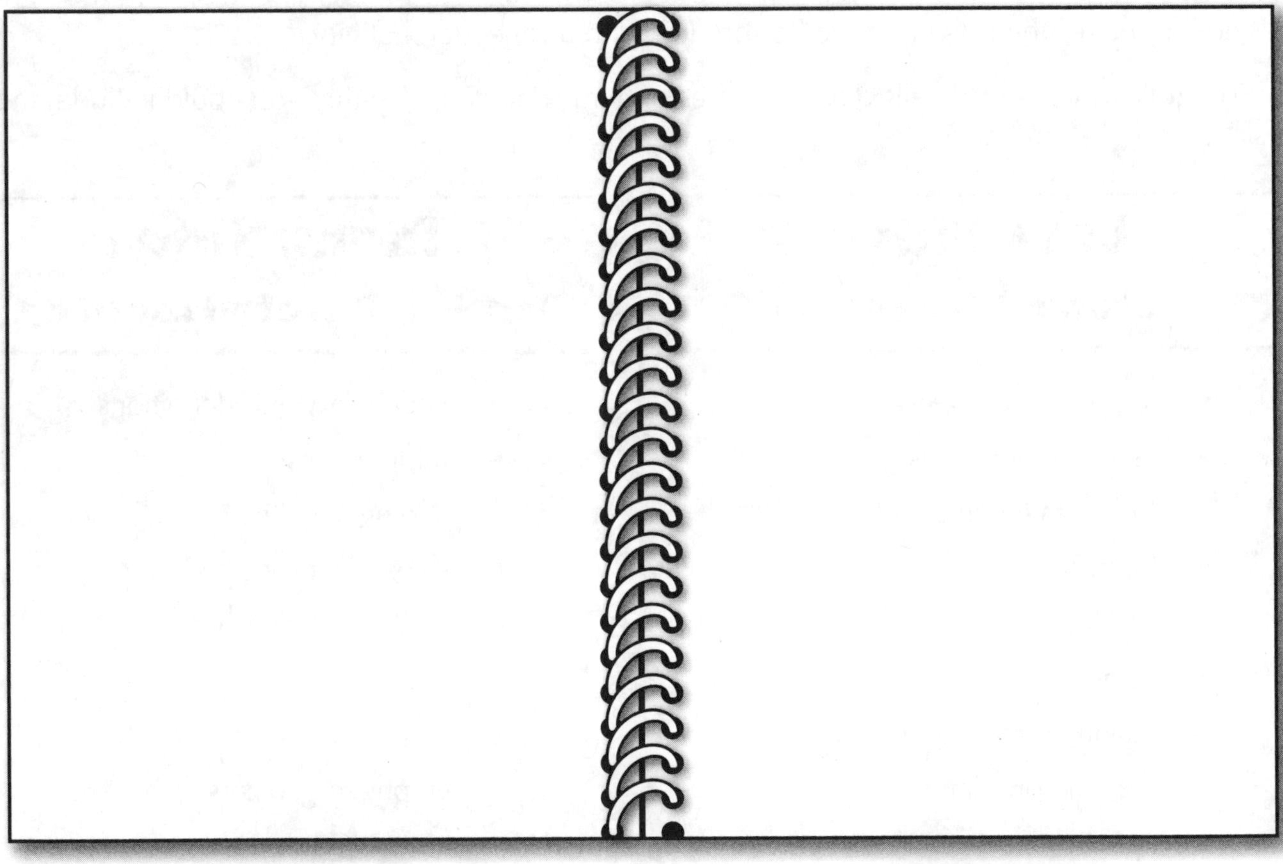

Left Side   **Right Side**

Notes

_____

_____

_____

Interactive Notebook Plan

Page	Topic	Page	Topic
1		51	
2		52	
3		53	
4		54	
5		55	
6		56	
7		57	
8		58	
9		59	
10		60	
11		61	
12		62	
13		63	
14		64	
15		65	
16		66	
17		67	
18		68	
19		69	
20		70	
21		71	
22		72	
23		73	
24		74	
25		75	
26		76	
27		77	
28		78	
29		79	
30		80	
31		81	
32		82	
33		83	
34		84	
35		85	
36		86	
37		87	
38		88	
39		89	
40		90	
41		91	
42		92	
43		93	
44		94	
45		95	
46		96	
47		97	
48		98	
49		99	
50		100	

Managing Interactive Notebooks in the Classroom

Working with Younger Students

- Use your yearly plan to preprogram a table of contents that you can copy and give to students to glue into their notebooks, instead of writing individual entries.

- Have assistants or parent volunteers precut pieces.

- Create glue sponges to make gluing easier. Place large sponges in plastic containers with white glue. The sponges will absorb the glue. Students can wipe the backs of pieces across the sponges to apply the glue with less mess.

Creating Notebook Pages

- For storing loose pieces, add a pocket to the inside back cover. Use the envelope pattern (page 81), an envelope, or a resealable plastic bag. Or, tape the bottom and side edges of the two last pages of the notebook together to create a large pocket.

- When writing under flaps, have students trace the outline of each flap so that they can visualize the writing boundary.

- Where the dashed line will be hidden on the inside of the fold, have students first fold the piece in the opposite direction so that they can see the dashed line. Then, students should fold the piece back the other way along the same fold line to create the fold in the correct direction.

- To avoid losing pieces, have students keep all of their scraps on their desks until they have finished each page.

- To contain paper scraps and avoid multiple trips to the trash can, provide small groups with small buckets or tubs.

- For students who run out of room, keep full and half sheets available. Students can glue these to the bottom of the pages and fold them up when not in use.

Dealing with Absences

- Create a model notebook for absent students to reference when they return to school.

- Have students cut a second set of pieces as they work on their own pages.

Using the Notebook

- To organize sections of the notebook, provide each student with a sheet of tabs (page 78).

- To easily find the next blank page, either cut off the top-right corner of each page as it is used or attach a long piece of yarn or ribbon to the back cover to be used as a bookmark.

Interactive Notebook Grading Rubric

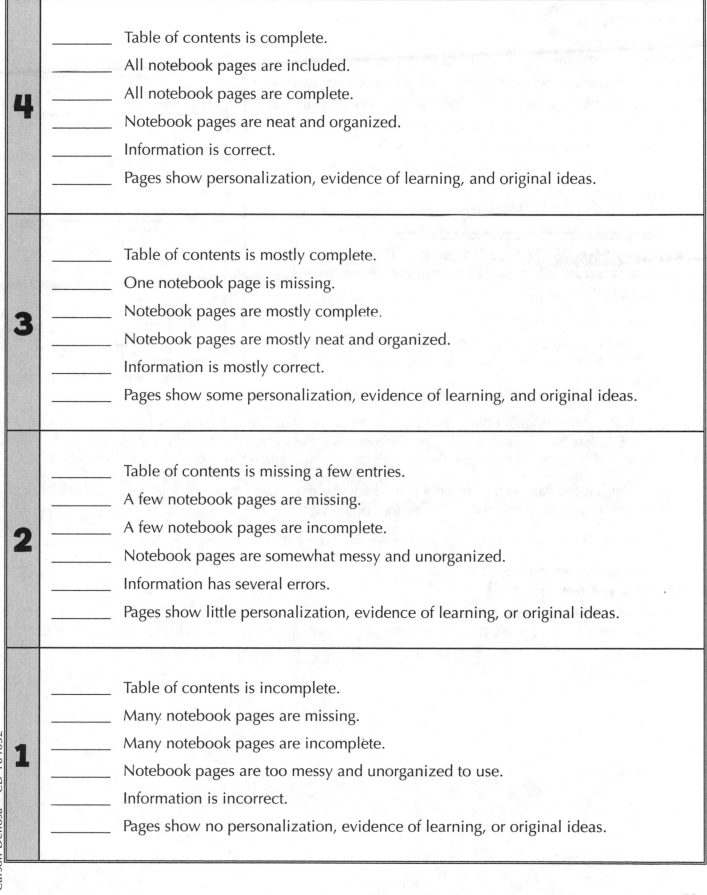

4
- _____ Table of contents is complete.
- _____ All notebook pages are included.
- _____ All notebook pages are complete.
- _____ Notebook pages are neat and organized.
- _____ Information is correct.
- _____ Pages show personalization, evidence of learning, and original ideas.

3
- _____ Table of contents is mostly complete.
- _____ One notebook page is missing.
- _____ Notebook pages are mostly complete.
- _____ Notebook pages are mostly neat and organized.
- _____ Information is mostly correct.
- _____ Pages show some personalization, evidence of learning, and original ideas.

2
- _____ Table of contents is missing a few entries.
- _____ A few notebook pages are missing.
- _____ A few notebook pages are incomplete.
- _____ Notebook pages are somewhat messy and unorganized.
- _____ Information has several errors.
- _____ Pages show little personalization, evidence of learning, or original ideas.

1
- _____ Table of contents is incomplete.
- _____ Many notebook pages are missing.
- _____ Many notebook pages are incomplete.
- _____ Notebook pages are too messy and unorganized to use.
- _____ Information is incorrect.
- _____ Pages show no personalization, evidence of learning, or original ideas.

Consonants and Vowels

Introduction

Explain that consonants are speech sounds that are not vowels. They also represent 21 letters of the alphabet that are not vowels. Review the sounds that each of the consonants make. Explain that five of the letters in the alphabet create vowel sounds. Review the letters *a*, *e*, *i*, *o*, and *u*. Write a word on the board. Have a volunteer come to the board and read the word. Then, have him circle the consonant(s) and underline the vowel(s). Repeat the activity several times with different words.

Creating the Notebook Page

Guide students through the following steps to complete the right-hand page in their notebooks.

1. Add a Table of Contents entry for the Consonants and Vowels pages.

2. Cut out the title and glue it to the top of the page.

3. Cut out the alphabet piece and glue it below the title. Complete the explanation. (There are **26** letters in the alphabet. Twenty-one letters make **consonant** sounds. Five letters make **vowel** sounds.) Next, circle the consonants and underline the vowels in the alphabet.

4. Cut out the flap book. Cut on the solid line to create two flaps. Apply glue to the back of the top section and attach it to the bottom of the page.

5. Write the vowels and consonants under the correct flaps.

Reflect on Learning

To complete the left-hand page, have students write various words such as weekly spelling words or sight words. Have students circle the consonants and underline the vowels in each word.

Consonants and Vowels

There are _____ letters in the alphabet.

Twenty-one letters make _____ sounds.

Five letters make _____ sounds.

a b c d e f g h i j k l m
n o p q r s t u v w x y z

I know my **consonants** and **vowels**!

Vowels

Consonants

Short Vowel Sounds

This lesson is designed to introduce one or more vowel sounds at a time and can be taught over several days.

Introduction

Introduce each short vowel. For each vowel sound, display a short poem or song with a repeated short vowel sound, such as "Where is Short A?" (sung to the tune of "Where is Thumbkin?"). Encourage students to brainstorm a list of words with the short vowel sound introduced. Write the words on the board as students say them.

Creating the Notebook Page

Guide students through the following steps to complete the right-hand page in their notebooks.

1. Add a Table of Contents entry for the Short Vowel Sounds pages.

2. Cut out the title and glue it to the top of the page.

3. Cut out the flaps. Apply glue to the back of the top section of each flap and attach it to the page.

4. Draw pictures or write words under each flap to represent each short vowel sound.

Reflect on Learning

To complete the left-hand page, have students make a vowel collage. Provide students with magazines and newspapers. Have students choose a vowel sound and then cut out pictures and words with the chosen sound. Have students glue the pictures and words in a collage format. Allow time for students to share their work.

Short Vowel Sounds

Vowel Teams: Long *a*

Students will need a sharpened pencil and a paper clip to complete the spinner activity.

Introduction

Write the word *bat* on the board. Write the word *bait* beside it. Say the words. Ask students what they notice about the two words. Explain that the long vowel sound *a* can be made by combining two vowels. This is called a *vowel team* because the vowels work together to make the long vowel sound. Explain the rhyme "When two vowels go walking, the first one does the talking." Write a few more words such as *pad/paid* and *man/main.* Have students read, then say the words. Have volunteers come to the board and circle the vowel team in each word.

Creating the Notebook Page

Guide students through the following steps to complete the right-hand page in their notebooks.

1. Add a Table of Contents entry for the Vowel Teams: Long *a* pages.

2. Cut out the title and glue it to the top of the page.

3. Cut out the word bank and glue it to the top-left side of the page.

4. Cut out the spinner and glue it beside the word bank.

5. Cut out the flap book. Cut on the solid lines to create two flaps. Apply glue to the back of the top section and attach it to the bottom of the page.

6. Use a sharpened pencil and a paper clip to spin the spinner. Choose a word from the word bank that matches the vowel team spun. Write it under the correct flap. Highlight the vowel team in each word.

7. Continue the activity until all of the words from the word bank have been used.

Reflect on Learning

To complete the left-hand page, have students brainstorm more words with the vowel teams *ai* and *ay.* Then, have them write short poems using words from their lists and the word bank. Allow time for students to share their work.

Vowel Teams: Long *a*

Word Bank

chain	clay
drain	day
maid	lay
paint	pay
rain	play
sail	tray
wait	way

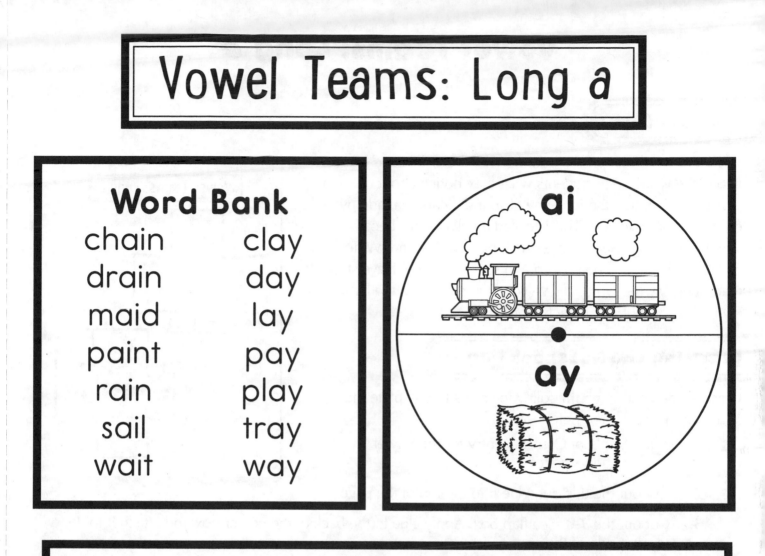

When two vowels go walking, the first one does the talking!

Vowel Teams: Long *e*

Introduction

Write the word *seat* on the board. Write the word *seed* beside it. Say the words. Ask students what they notice about the two words. Explain that the long vowel sound *e* can be made by combining two vowels. This is called a *vowel team* because the vowels work together to make the long vowel sound. Write a few more words such as *heat/heed* and *scream/screen*. Have students read, then say the words. Have volunteers come to the board and circle the vowel team in each word.

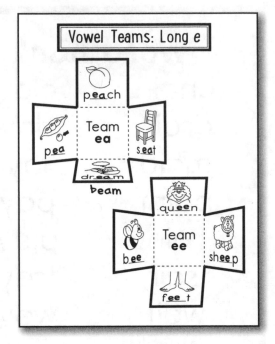

Creating the Notebook Page

Guide students through the following steps to complete the right-hand page in their notebooks.

1. Add a Table of Contents entry for the Vowel Teams: Long *e* pages.

2. Cut out the title and glue it to the top of the page.

3. Cut out the *Team ea* flap box. Apply glue to the back of the center box and attach it to the top-left side of the page.

4. Complete the words on the top of each flap by writing *ea* in each of the blanks.

5. Write a word with the same vowel team under each flap. Highlight the vowel team in each word.

6. Repeat steps 3–5 with the *Team ee* flap box, attaching the back of the center box to the bottom-right side of the page.

Reflect on Learning

To complete the left-hand page, have students choose six of the words from the right-hand page. Then, have them write short sentences with each of the words. Have students highlight the vowel team in each word used.

Vowel Teams: Long *e*

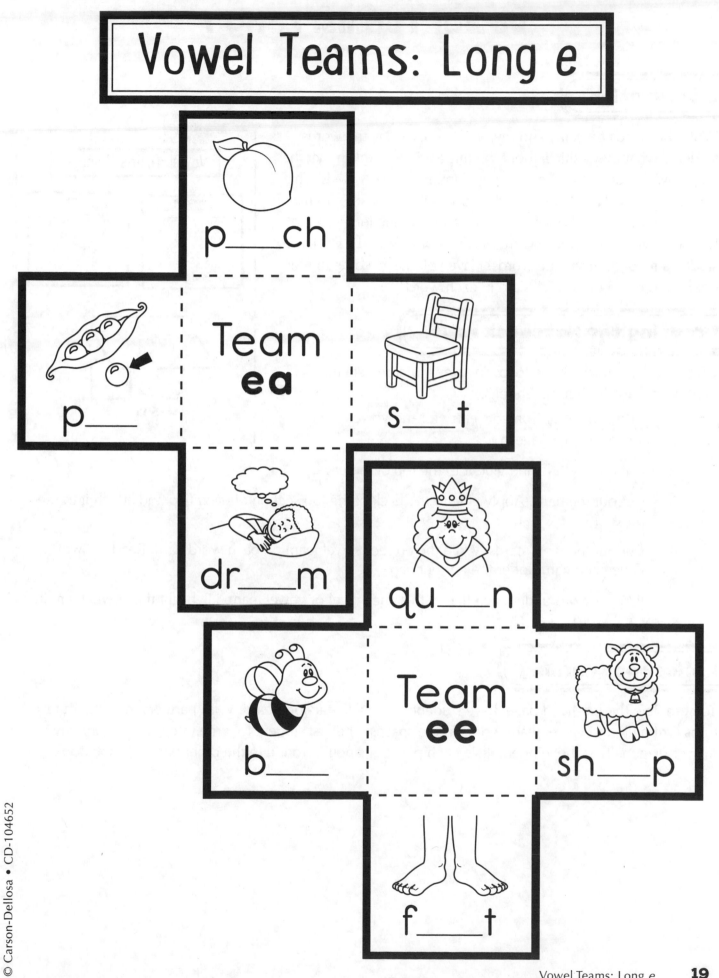

p___ch

Team
ea

p___

s___t

dr___m

qu___n

Team
ee

b___

sh___p

f___t

Vowel Teams: Long *i*

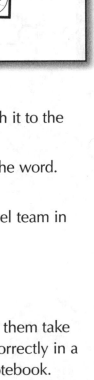

Vowel Teams: Long *i*

Team **ie**

Team **igh**

Team **y**

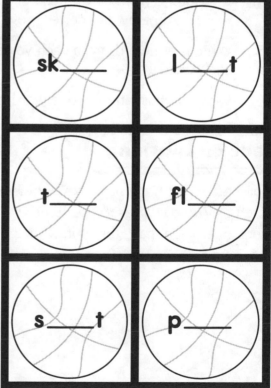

sk____

l____t

t____

fl____

s____t

p____

Vowel Teams: Long *o*

Introduction

Write the words *tow* and *float* on the board. Say the words. Ask students what they notice about the two words. Explain that the long vowel sound *o* can be made by combining two vowels. This is called a *vowel team* because the vowels work together to make the long vowel sound. Write a few more words such as *snow* and *soap*. Have students read, then say the words. Have volunteers come to the board and circle the vowel team in each word.

Creating the Notebook Page

Guide students through the following steps to complete the right-hand page in their notebooks.

1. Add a Table of Contents entry for the Vowel Teams: Long *o* pages.

2. Cut out the title and glue it to the top of the page.

3. Cut out the flap book. Cut on the solid line to create two flaps. Apply glue to the back of the top section and attach it below the title.

4. Cut out the word cards. Read each word. Highlight the vowel team in each word. Glue each word card below the correct vowel team.

5. Write more words from each vowel team under the flaps. Highlight the vowel team in each word.

6. Draw an illustration of one word from the vowel team below each flap.

Reflect on Learning

To complete the left-hand page, have students write a silly sentence using words from the right-hand page such as *The goat likes to float on the boat.* Have students highlight the *oa* and *ow* words used in each sentence. Then, have them draw pictures to illustrate the sentences. Allow time for students to share their work.

Vowel Teams: Long *o*

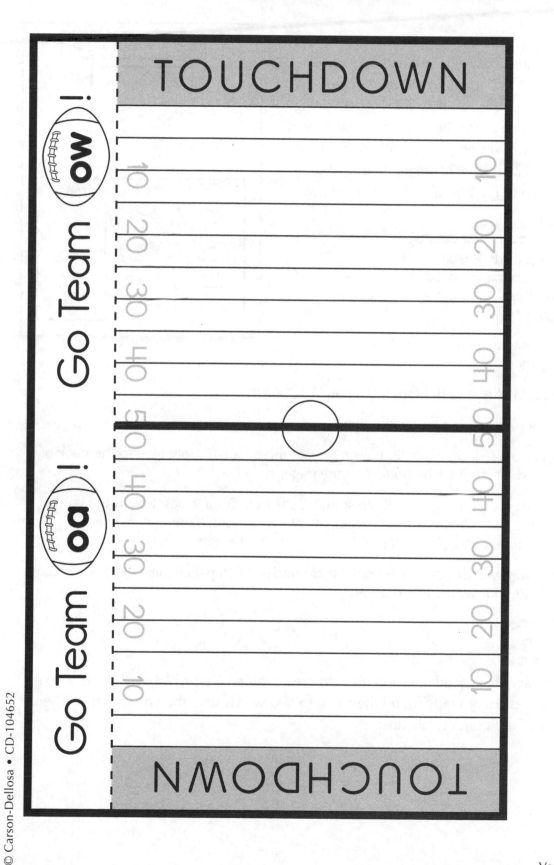

TOUCHDOWN

ow

Go Team ow!

10 20 30 40 50 40 30 20 10

oa

Go Team oa!

TOUCHDOWN

goat

soap

glow

float

snow

row

boat

throw

show

road

Vowel Teams: Long *u*

Students will need a sharpened pencil and a paper clip to complete the spinner activity.

Introduction

Write the words *clue*, *juice*, and *chew* on the board. Say the words. Ask students what they notice about the three words. Explain that the long vowel sound *u* can be made by combining two vowels. This is called a *vowel team* because the vowels work together to make the long vowel sound. Write a few more words such as *due*, *fruit*, and *blew*. Have students read, then say the words. Have volunteers come to the board and circle the vowel team in each word.

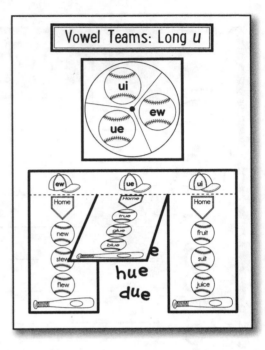

Creating the Notebook Page

Guide students through the following steps to complete the right-hand page in their notebooks.

1. Add a Table of Contents entry for the Vowel Teams: Long *u* pages.

2. Cut out the title and glue it to the top of the page.

3. Cut out the spinner and glue it below the title.

4. Cut out the flap book. Cut on the solid lines to create three flaps. Apply glue to the back of the top section and attach it to the bottom of the page.

5. Use a sharpened pencil and a paper clip to spin the spinner. Color a baseball in the correct column each time a vowel team is spun, beginning at the bottom. Continue spinning and coloring baseballs until one column of baseballs has reached a home plate.

6. Practice writing more words from each vowel team under the flaps. Highlight the vowel team in each word. Read your words to a partner.

Reflect on Learning

To complete the left-hand page, have students draw lines to create three columns labeled *ui*, *ue*, and *ew*. Have students look through books or read around the room to find words with the vowel teams. Then, have them write the words in the correct columns.

© Carson-Dellosa • CD-104652

Vowel Teams: Long *u*

ew

Home

new

stew

flew

ue

Home

true

glue

blue

ui

Home

fruit

suit

juice

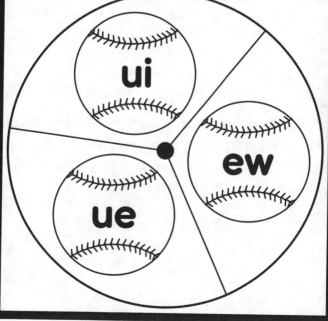

ui

ew

ue

Final Silent e

Introduction

Write the words *pan*, *bit*, *rip*, *not*, *ton*, *tub*, and *cub* in a column on the board. As a class, read the words aloud. Then, have the students close their eyes. Add an *e* to each word. Explain that "sneaky *e*" silently sneaks in and turns the short vowel sound in each word into a long vowel sound. Remind students that the *e* is silent. Have students read the new words aloud.

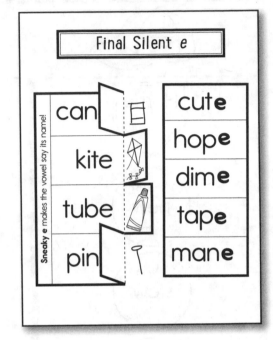

Creating the Notebook Page

Guide students through the following steps to complete the right-hand page in their notebooks.

1. Add a Table of Contents entry for the Final Silent *e* pages.

2. Cut out the title and glue it to the top of the page.

3. Cut out the *Sneaky e* flap book. Cut on the solid lines to create four flaps. Apply glue to the back of the left section and attach it to the left side of the page.

4. Practice reading the words with and without the silent *e* by covering and uncovering the "sneaky *e*" back and forth along the dashed line.

5. Draw a picture of the new word that is made without the final *e* under each flap.

6. Cut out the five-word card piece and glue it to the right side of the page.

7. Cut out the magnifying glass. Read each word. Then, move it along the word card and practice reading the new words made with the "sneaky *e*." Write the final *e* at the end of each word after the word is read.

Reflect on Learning

To complete the left-hand page, have students draw lines to divide their pages into four squares labeled *long a*, *long i*, *long o*, and *long u*. Then, have them draw pictures of objects (Examples: a cake, a kite, a robe, a tube) in each square that use the final silent *e* to change the short vowel sound to a long vowel sound. Then, have students write the word under each object.

Final Silent *e*

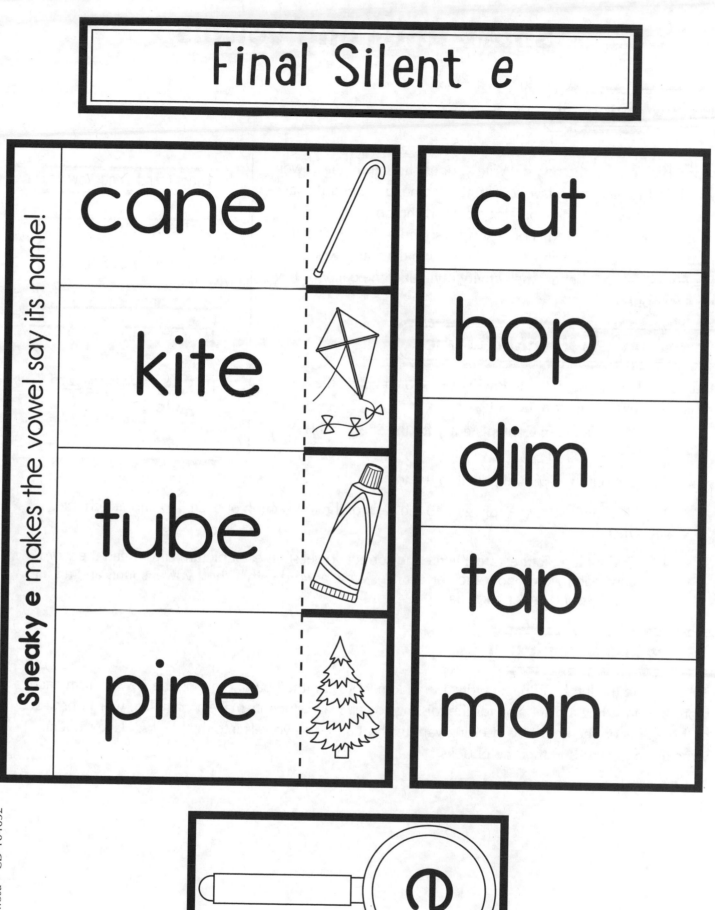

Sneaky e makes the vowel say its name!

cane	
kite	
tube	
pine	

cut
hop
dim
tap
man

Short and Long Vowels

Introduction

Review short and long vowel sounds with a game. Draw 10 (or more) balloons on the board. Write various short and long vowel words in the balloons. Have a volunteer come to the board. Have her "pop" a balloon that contains a certain short or long vowel sound. For example, say, "Pop a short *e* sound balloon." The student will then draw an "X" over a balloon that has a word with the correct sound. Repeat the activity until all of the balloons have been "popped."

Creating the Notebook Page

Guide students through the following steps to complete the right-hand page in their notebooks.

1. Add a Table of Contents entry for the Short and Long Vowels pages.

2. Cut out the title and glue it to the top of the page.

3. Cut out the flaps. Apply glue to the back of the top section of each flap and attach it to the page.

4. Cut out the picture cards. Write the correct vowel(s) on each picture card. Read the word. Glue each word under the correct flap. Write a word with a short vowel sound and a long vowel sound under each flap.

Reflect on Learning

To complete the left-hand page, write 15 random words on the board, omitting the vowels from each word and inserting a blank line for the missing vowel. Have students make a complete word from each of the words on the board by inserting various short and long vowels into the blanks. Have students write the new words in their notebooks.

Short and Long Vowels

I know my **short vowel** sounds!

Short Vowel Sounds

I know my **long vowel** sounds!

Long Vowel Sounds

| __ce | d__sk | g__t | b__ll | dr__m |
| g__m | k__t__ | t__st | d__c__ | k__ng |

Consonant Blends: s

Introduction

Draw a large bowl on the board. Write *scale*, *swan*, *spider*, *snake*, *stamp*, and *skate* in the "bowl." Discuss how things that blend are mixed together. A consonant blend is two or more consonants blended together to make one sound. Point to each word in the bowl. Explain that each word begins with a consonant *s* blend. Have volunteers come to the board, say each word, and underline the consonant blend.

Creating the Notebook Page

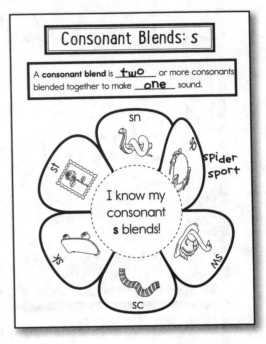

Guide students through the following steps to complete the right-hand page in their notebooks.

1. Add a Table of Contents entry for the Consonant Blends: *s* pages.

2. Cut out the title and glue it to the top of the page.

3. Cut out the definition box. Glue it below the title. Complete the definition of a consonant blend. (A **consonant blend** is **two** or more consonants blended together to make **one** sound.)

4. Cut out the flower piece. Cut on the solid lines to create six petal-shaped flaps. Apply glue to the back of the center section and attach it to the page.

5. Look at the pictures on each petal. Say the word the picture represents.

6. Write the correct word under each petal. Then, write another word with the same consonant *s* blend under the petal.

Reflect on Learning

To complete the left-hand page, have students brainstorm a list of *s* blend words. Write the words on the board as they say them. Then, have students number their pages from 1 to 10. Give a riddle for 10 of the consonant *s* blend words that are written on the board. For example, if *string* is written on the board say, "This is something you tie to a kite so you can fly it." Have students write the correct word in their notebooks as they solve the riddles.

Consonant Blends: s

A **consonant blend** is _____ or more consonants blended together to make _____ sound.

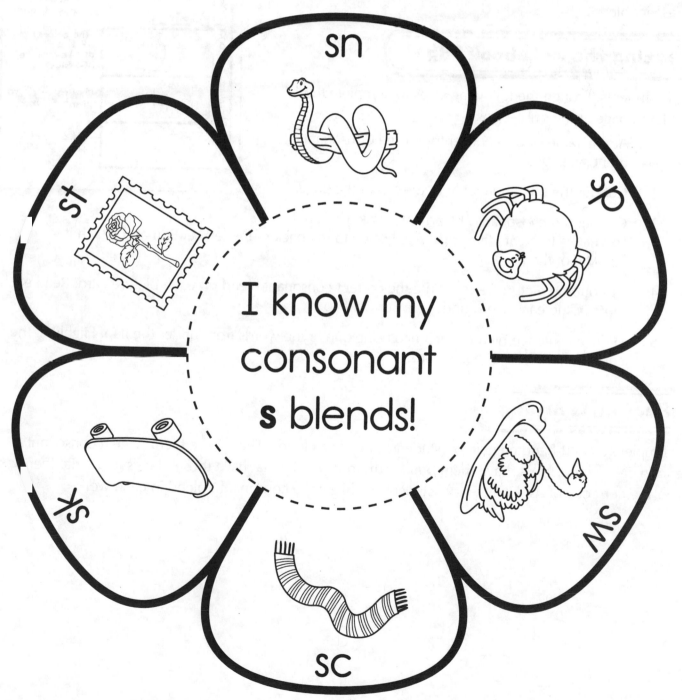

sn

sp

sw

sc

sk

st

I know my consonant **s** blends!

Consonant Blends: *l*

Introduction

Draw a large bowl on the board. Write *blank*, *clue*, *flew*, *place*, and *slim* in the "bowl." Discuss how things that blend are mixed together. A consonant blend is two or more consonants blended together to make one sound. Point to each word in the bowl. Explain that each word begins with a consonant *l* blend. Have volunteers come to the board, say each word, and underline the consonant blend.

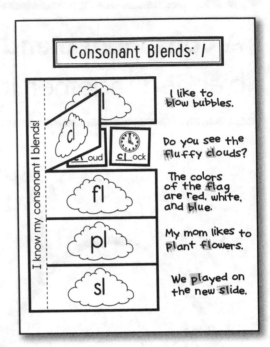

Creating the Notebook Page

Guide students through the following steps to complete the right-hand page in their notebooks.

1. Add a Table of Contents entry for the Consonant Blends: *l* pages.

2. Cut out the title and glue it to the top of the page.

3. Cut out the consonant *l* blend flap book. Cut on the solid lines to create five flaps. Apply glue to the back of the left section and attach it to the left side of the page.

4. Cut out the picture cards. Write the correct consonant blend on each picture card. Read each word. Glue each word under the correct flap.

5. Write a sentence next to each flap using one of the words from under the flap. Highlight the consonant *l* blend in each word.

Reflect on Learning

To complete the left-hand page, have students draw five clouds. Then, have them write a consonant *l* blend in each cloud. Next, have them brainstorm more words that have those blends and write them under the correct clouds. Finally, have students highlight the consonant *l* blend in each word.

Consonant Blends: l

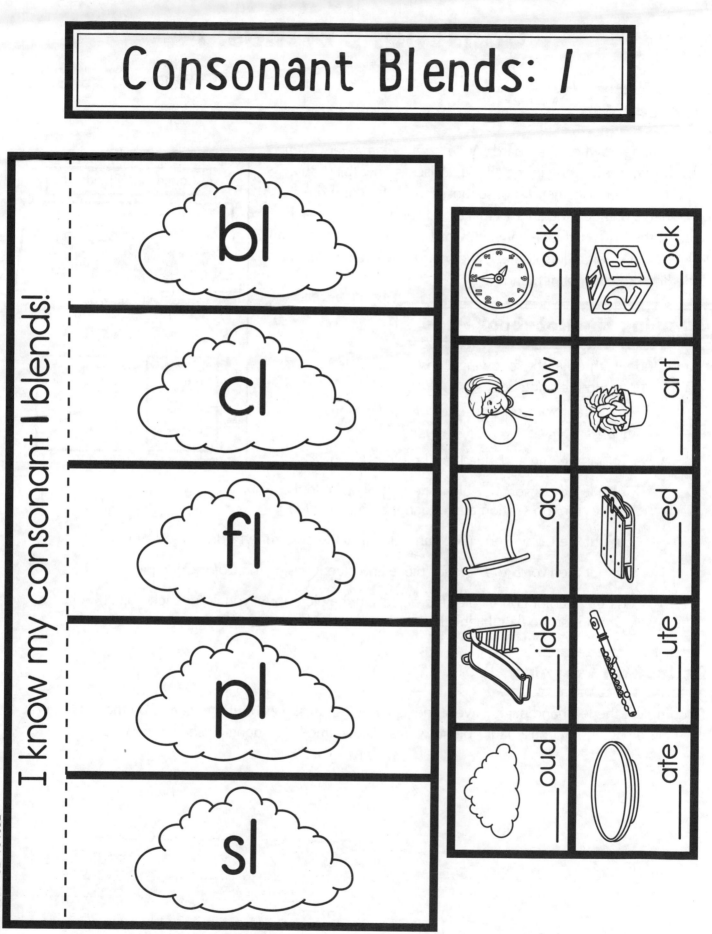

I know my consonant l blends!

bl

cl

fl

pl

sl

___ock

___ock

___ow

___ant

___ag

___ed

___ide

___ute

___oud

___ate

Consonant Blends: *r*

Introduction

Draw a large bowl on the board. Write *brim, cream, draw, frame, grab, proud,* and *trophy* in the "bowl." Discuss how things that blend are mixed together. A consonant blend is two or more consonants blended together to make one sound. Point to each word in the bowl. Explain that each word begins with a consonant *r* blend. Have volunteers come to the board, say each word, and underline the consonant blend.

Creating the Notebook Page

Guide students through the following steps to complete the right-hand page in their notebooks.

1. Add a Table of Contents entry for the Consonant Blends: *r* pages.

2. Cut out the title and glue it to the top of the page.

3. Cut out the consonant *r* blend flap. Apply glue to the back of the top section and attach it below the title.

4. Cut out the *Color Code* piece and glue it to the bottom-left side of the page.

5. Cut out the *Words to Look For* piece and glue it beside the *Color Code* piece.

6. Using the color code, color the objects in the picture. As you color each object, write the word under the flap. Highlight the consonant *r* blend in each word.

Reflect on Learning

To complete the left-hand page, have students write a short story about the picture on the right-hand side of the page using consonant *r* blend words. Allow time for students to share their work.

Consonant Blends: *r*

I know my consonant **r** blends!

crow   truck

Color Code		Words to Look For	
br = orange		broom	frog
cr = yellow		crab	grapes
dr = blue		crow	grill
fr = green		crown	pretzel
gr = purple		dress	prize
pr = brown		drum	truck
tr = red			

Consonant Blends: r

I know my consonant r blends!

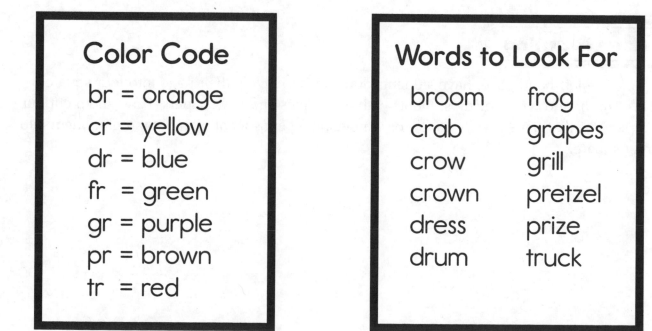

Color Code

br = orange
cr = yellow
dr = blue
fr = green
gr = purple
pr = brown
tr = red

Words to Look For

broom	frog
crab	grapes
crow	grill
crown	pretzel
dress	prize
drum	truck

Beginning Consonant Digraphs

Introduction

Write several *ch*, *sh*, *th*, and *wh* beginning consonant digraph words on the board. Say the words aloud. Explain that a consonant digraph combines two consonant sounds to make a new sound. Discuss how the consonant digraph in each word produces the new sound at the beginning. Ask students to give more examples of words with beginning consonant digraphs. Write them on the board as students say them. Have volunteers come to the board and underline the beginning consonant digraphs in each word.

Creating the Notebook Page

Guide students through the following steps to complete the right-hand page in their notebooks.

1. Add a Table of Contents entry for the Beginning Consonant Digraphs pages.

2. Cut out the title and glue it to the top of the page.

3. Cut out the flap book. Cut on the solid lines to create two flaps on each side. Apply glue to the back of the center section and attach it to the page.

4. Cut out the picture cards. Write the correct beginning consonant digraph on each picture card. Read each word. Glue each word under the correct flap.

5. Write or draw another word with a beginning consonant digraph under each flap.

Reflect on Learning

To complete the left-hand page, have students draw lines to divide their page into four squares labeled *ch*, *sh*, *th*, and *wh*. Provide students with magazines and newspapers. Have them cut out words or pictures that have the *ch*, *sh*, *th*, or *wh* beginning consonant digraph and glue them into the correct square.

Beginning Consonant Digraphs

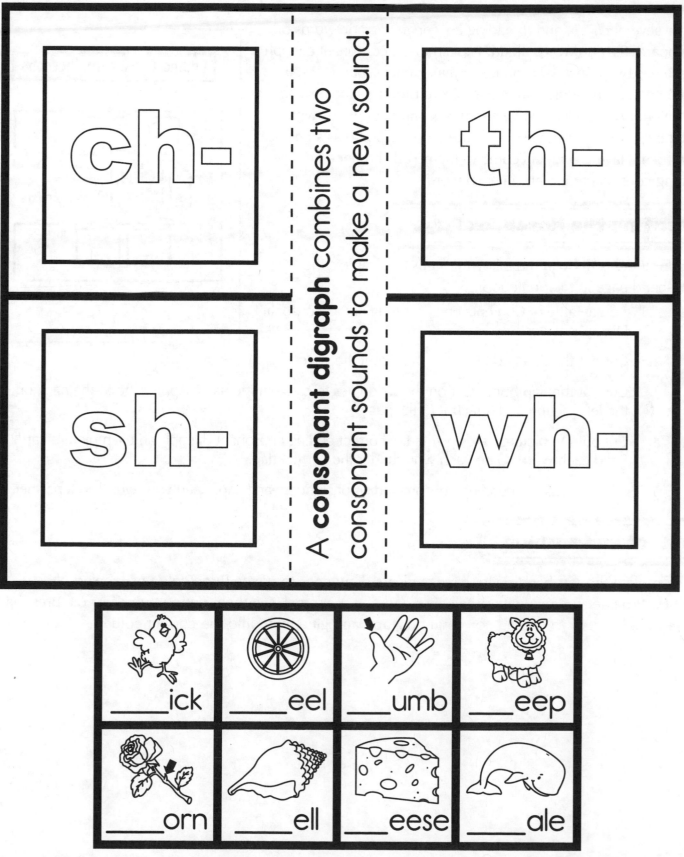

ch-

th-

sh-

wh-

A **consonant digraph** combines two consonant sounds to make a new sound.

____ick ____eel ____umb ____eep

____orn ____ell ____eese ____ale

Ending Consonant Digraphs

Introduction

Write several *ch*, *sh*, and *th* ending consonant digraph words on the board. Say the words aloud. Explain that a consonant digraph combines two consonant sounds to make a new sound. Discuss how the consonant digraph in each word produces the new sound at the end. Ask students to give more examples of words with ending consonant digraphs. Write them on the board as students say them. Have volunteers come to the board and underline the ending consonant digraphs in each word.

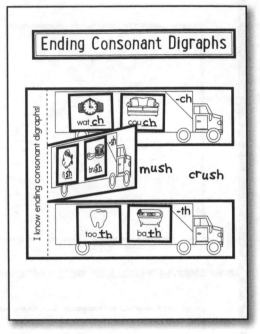

Creating the Notebook Page

Guide students through the following steps to complete the right-hand page in their notebooks.

1. Add a Table of Contents entry for the Ending Consonant Digraphs pages.

2. Cut out the title and glue it to the top of the page.

3. Cut out the flap book. Cut on the solid lines to create three flaps. Apply glue to the back of the left section and attach it to the page.

4. Cut out the picture cards. Write the correct ending consonant digraph on each picture card. Read each word. Glue each word under the correct flap.

5. Write words with ending consonant digraphs under each flap. Read your words to a partner.

Reflect on Learning

To complete the left-hand page, have students draw lines to create three columns labeled *ch*, *sh*, and *th*. Provide students with magazines and newspapers. Have them cut out words or pictures that have the *ch*, *sh*, or *th* ending consonant digraph and glue them into the correct columns.

Ending Consonant Digraphs

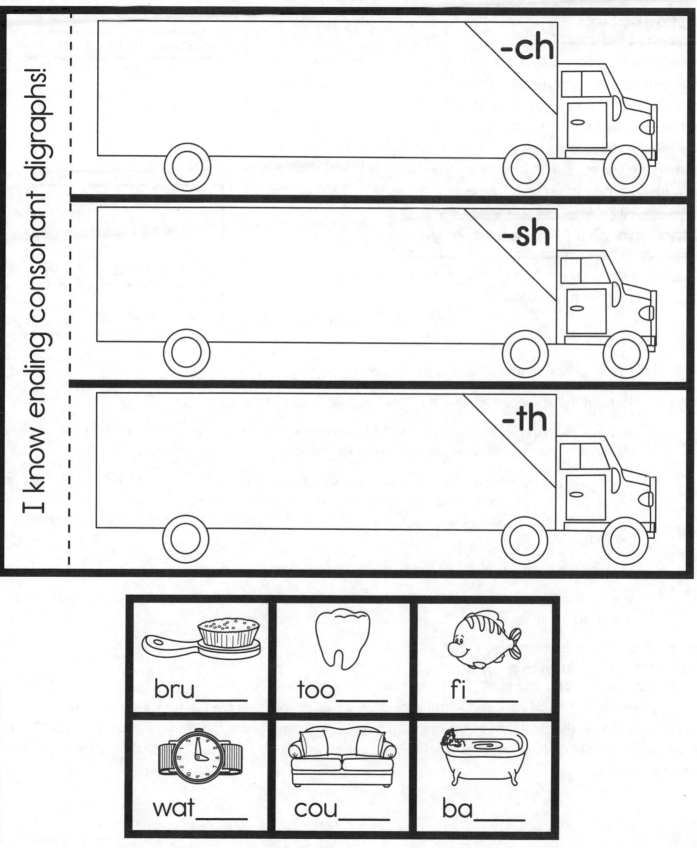

I know ending consonant digraphs!

-ch

-sh

-th

bru____   too____   fi____

wat____   cou____   ba____

Consonant Digraphs Review

Students will need a sharpened pencil and a paper clip to complete the spinner activity.

Introduction

Provide each student with a self-stick note that has either a beginning or ending consonant digraph word written on it. Have students highlight the digraph in their words. Draw two circles on the board. Label the circles *Beginning Digraph* and *Ending Digraph*. Have students bring their words to the board and place them in the correct circle. As a class, read the words and decide if they are placed in the correct circles.

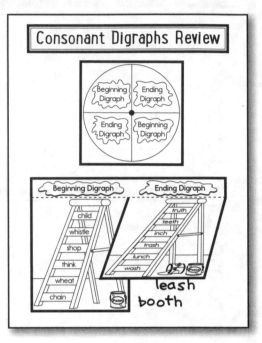

Creating the Notebook Page

Guide students through the following steps to complete the right-hand page in their notebooks.

1. Add a Table of Contents entry for the Consonant Diagraphs Review pages.

2. Cut out the title and glue it to the top of the page.

3. Cut out the spinner and glue it below the title.

4. Cut out the flap book. Cut on the solid line to create two flaps. Apply glue to the back of the top section and attach it to the bottom of the page.

5. Use a sharpened pencil and a paper clip to spin the spinner. If the spinner lands on *Beginning Digraph*, color a word on the *Beginning Digraph* ladder beginning at the bottom. If the spinner lands on *Ending Digraph*, color a word on the *Ending Digraph* ladder beginning at the bottom.

6. Continue spinning until all of the words on one ladder are colored in.

7. Practice writing more words with beginning and ending digraphs under each flap. Read your words to a partner.

Reflect on Learning

To complete the left-hand page, have students draw a beach scene. Have them include objects that might be found on the beach or in the water that have beginning or ending digraph sounds such as *shark teeth*, *fish*, and *shells*. Have students label the digraph words in each picture. Allow time for students to share their work.

Consonant Digraphs Review

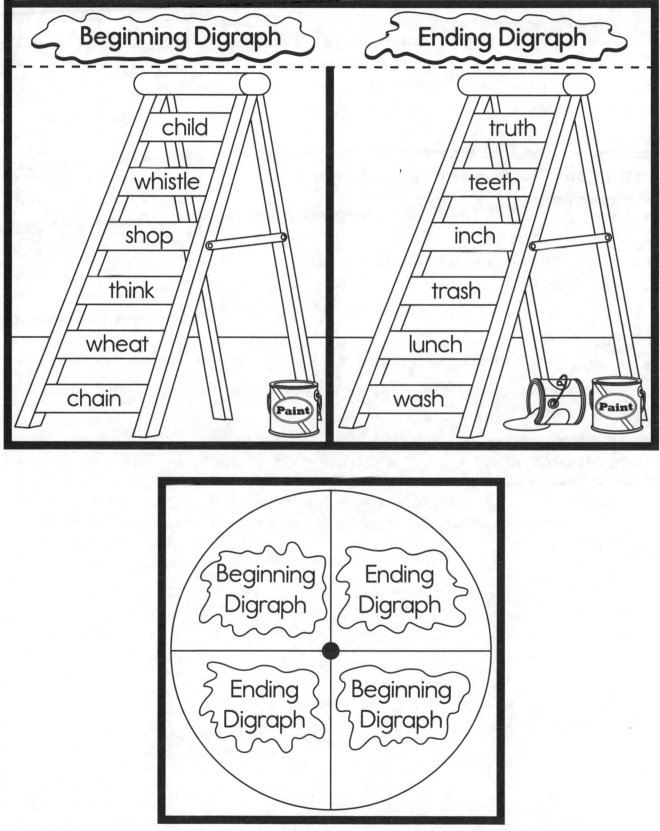

Beginning Digraph

child
whistle
shop
think
wheat
chain

Ending Digraph

truth
teeth
inch
trash
lunch
wash

Paint

Beginning Digraph

Ending Digraph

Ending Digraph

Beginning Digraph

Rhyming Words

Introduction

Explain that words that have the same ending sound are called *rhyming words*. The beginning sounds of the words are usually different. Write a word on the board such as *cake*. Have a volunteer write a word that rhymes with *cake*, such as *bake*. Continue this several times with different words. As a class, compose a short poem that contains rhyming words. Have volunteers circle the rhyming words in the poem.

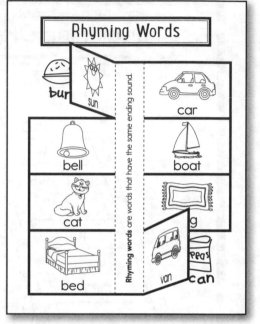

Creating the Notebook Page

Guide students through the following steps to complete the right-hand page in their notebooks.

1. Add a Table of Contents entry for the Rhyming Words pages.

2. Cut out the title and glue it to the top of the page.

3. Cut out the flap book. Cut on the solid lines to create four flaps on each side. Apply glue to the back of the center section and attach it to the page.

4. Read the word on each flap. Under the flap, write a word that rhymes with the word. Then, draw the word.

Reflect on Learning

To complete the left-hand page, have students write as many pairs of rhyming words as they can think of. Then, have students write and illustrate a short poem using some of the words. Allow time for students to share their work.

Rhyming Words

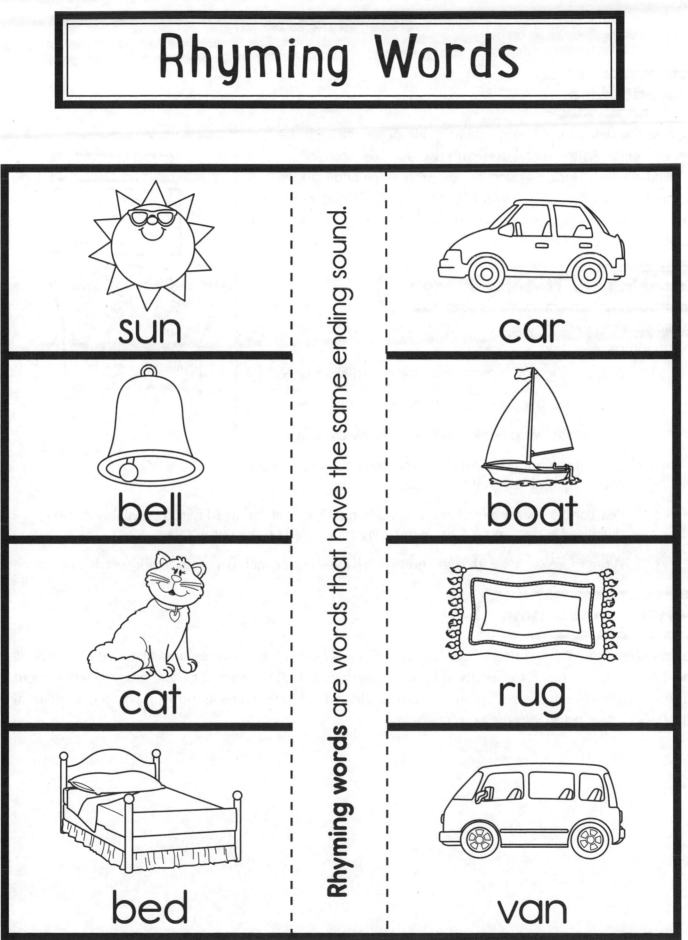

sun

bell

cat

bed

Rhyming words are words that have the same ending sound.

car

boat

rug

van

Syllables

Introduction

Discuss the definition of a syllable as a unit of speech with one vowel sound. Write several one- and two-syllable words on the board. Have students listen as you pronounce and clap the number of syllables in each word. Then, have each student say his name aloud and clap the syllables of his name. Have students clap out other words to hear how many syllables each word has.

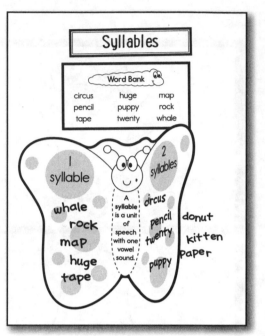

Creating the Notebook Page

Guide students through the following steps to complete the right-hand page in their notebooks.

1. Add a Table of Contents entry for the Syllables pages.

2. Cut out the title and glue it to the top of the page.

3. Cut out the word bank and glue it below the title.

4. Cut out the butterfly. Apply glue to the back of the head and body and attach it to the page.

5. Read and say each word in the word bank. Decide if the word has one syllable or two syllables by clapping out the word. Write the word on the correct flap.

6. Write more words with one and two syllables under each flap. Read your words to a partner.

Reflect on Learning

To complete the left-hand page, have students divide their page into two columns labeled *One Syllable* and *Two Syllables*. Instruct students to look through books to find words for each category. Have them write the words in the correct columns. Have students read their words aloud with partners to determine if the words are sorted into the correct columns.

Syllables

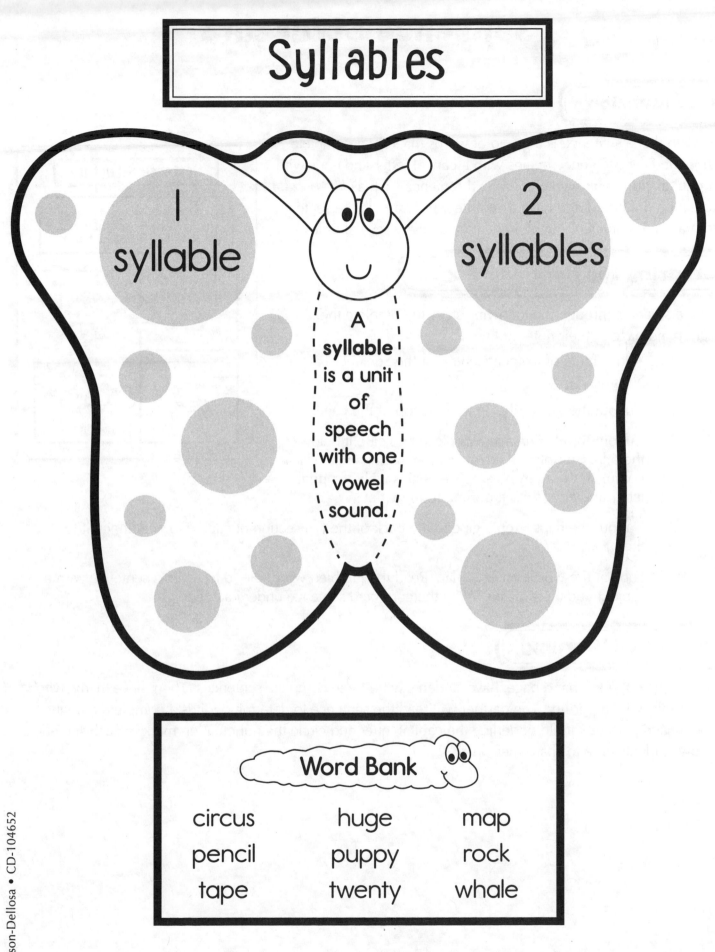

1 syllable

2 syllables

A **syllable** is a unit of speech with one vowel sound.

Word Bank

circus	huge	map
pencil	puppy	rock
tape	twenty	whale

Sentence Structure

Introduction

Explain that a sentence is a group of words that tells a complete thought. Every sentence begins with a capital letter and ends with a punctuation mark. Write a jumbled sentence such as *like pizza. I to eat* on the board and have a volunteer unscramble the sentence to make a complete thought. Repeat the activity several times.

Creating the Notebook Page

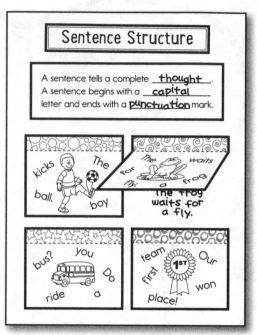

Guide students through the following steps to complete the right-hand page in their notebooks.

1. Add a Table of Contents entry for the Sentence Structure pages.

2. Cut out the title and glue it to the top of the page.

3. Cut out the *A sentence tells* piece and glue it below the title. Complete the explanation. (A sentence tells a complete **thought**. A sentence begins with a **capital** letter and ends with a **punctuation** mark.)

4. Cut out the flaps. Apply glue to the back of the top section of each flap and attach it to the page.

5. Look at the words on each flap. Read the jumbled words aloud to make a sentence with a subject and a predicate. Write the corrected sentence under each flap.

Reflect on Learning

To complete the left-hand page, have students write three complete sentences. Then, have them switch notebooks with a partner. The partner will read the sentence to determine if it is a complete thought. Then, each partner should underline the capital letter and circle the punctuation mark in each sentence. Allow students time to share their work.

Sentence Structure

A sentence tells a complete _____.
A sentence begins with a _____ letter and ends with a _____ mark.

Defining Words by Attributes

Introduction

Explain that attributes are characteristics of a person, place, or thing. They are words that describe an object. Read a riddle to students such as the following: *I can be red, yellow, or green. I grow on a tree. I am sweet and juicy. What am I?* Ask students what attributes they heard in the riddle. Write them on the board. Have students solve the riddle by thinking about the attributes described. Repeat the activity with another riddle.

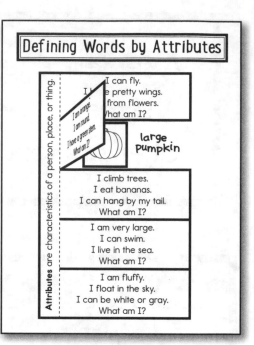

Creating the Notebook Page

Guide students through the following steps to complete the right-hand page in their notebooks.

1. Add a Table of Contents entry for the Defining Words by Attributes pages.

2. Cut out the title and glue it to the top of the page.

3. Cut out the flap book. Cut on the solid lines to create five flaps. Apply glue to the back of the left section and attach it to the page.

4. Cut out the picture cards.

5. Read each riddle. Decide which picture card answers the riddle. Glue the card under the correct flap. Write at least one more attribute for the object under each flap.

Reflect on Learning

To complete the left-hand page, have students write their own riddles. Then, have them highlight the attributes used to describe the object of their riddles. Have students exchange notebooks with a partner to guess the riddles and write the answers.

Defining Words by Attributes

Attributes are characteristics of a person, place, or thing.

I can fly.
I have pretty wings.
I sip from flowers.
What am I?

I am orange.
I am round.
I have a green stem.
What am I?

I climb trees.
I eat bananas.
I can hang by my tail.
What am I?

I am very large.
I can swim.
I live in the sea.
What am I?

I am fluffy.
I float in the sky.
I can be white or gray.
What am I?

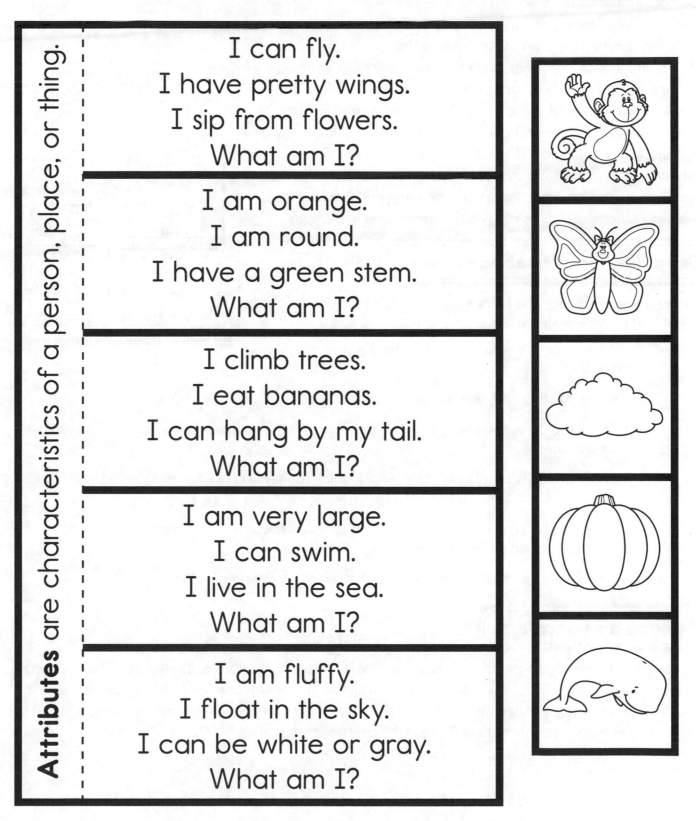

Prepositions

Introduction

Define a preposition as a word that shows the relationship between a noun or a pronoun to other words in the sentence. Write the following sentence on the board: *The dog is on the bed.* Circle the word *on.* Then, write *The dog is under the bed.* Circle the word *under.* Explain that the circled words are prepositions. Have a volunteer give another example of where the dog could be in relationship to the bed. Then, play a game of Simon Says using prepositions such as "Simon says put your hand *on top of* your head" or "Simon says put your pencil *behind* your back." Discuss the prepositional words or phrases that were used in the game.

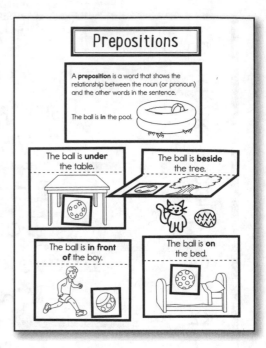

Creating the Notebook Page

Guide students through the following steps to complete the right-hand page in their notebooks.

1. Add a Table of Contents entry for the Prepositions pages.

2. Cut out the title and glue it to the top of the page.

3. Cut out the definition piece and glue it below the title. Discuss the meaning of the word *preposition.*

4. Cut out the flaps. Apply glue to the back of the top section of each flap and attach it to the page.

5. Cut out the ball pieces. For each flap, read the sentence, and then glue a ball in the appropriate place in the picture.

6. Draw another picture under each flap that illustrates the preposition.

Reflect on Learning

To complete the left-hand page, as a class, brainstorm a list of prepositions. Write them on the board as students say them. Then, have students draw a simple house. Then, have them add details to their houses such as drawing a tree beside the house or drawing a sun above the house. Have students label the prepositions shown. Allow time for students to share their work.

Prepositions

A **preposition** is a word that shows the relationship between the noun (or pronoun) and the other words in the sentence.

The ball is **in** the pool.

The ball is **under** the table.

The ball is **beside** the tree.

The ball is **in front of** the boy.

The ball is **on** the bed.

Common and Proper Nouns

Introduction

Review the definition of a noun as a word that describes a person, place, or thing. Explain that common nouns name general people, places, and things. Proper nouns name specific people, places, and things. Discuss how a proper noun begins with a capital letter. Write several examples of each type of noun on the board. Have volunteers come to the board and circle the common nouns and underline the proper nouns.

Creating the Notebook Page

Guide students through the following steps to complete the right-hand page in their notebooks.

1. Add a Table of Contents entry for the Common and Proper Nouns pages.

2. Cut out the title and glue it to the top of the page.

3. Cut out the flap book. Cut on the solid line to create two flaps. Apply glue to the back of the top section and attach it below the title.

4. Cut out the word cards. Read each one and decide if it is a proper noun or a common noun. Glue each card under the correct flap.

5. Write a sentence with a common noun or a sentence with a proper noun below each flap.

Reflect on Learning

To complete the left-hand page, have students draw lines to divide their page into two columns labeled *Common Nouns* and *Proper Nouns*. Send students on a scavenger hunt to look for common and proper nouns around the room or at home and record them in their notebooks.

Common and Proper Nouns

I know **common** and **proper nouns**!

Common Nouns

Proper Nouns

Ms. Taylor	New York	Murphy Lane	doctor
state	teacher	Dr. Lopez	street
June	month	fish	Goldie

Adjectives

Introduction

Review the definition of an adjective as a word that describes a noun. Discuss how adjectives can describe color, size, shape, or how many. Display a handful of gum balls to the class. Encourage students to describe them. Possible descriptions may include that the gum balls are small, round, and colorful. Write the adjectives on the board as students say them.

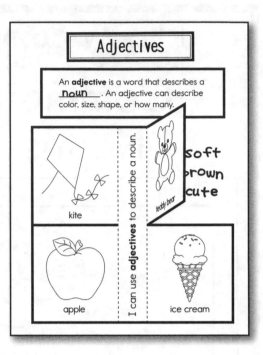

Creating the Notebook Page

Guide students through the following steps to complete the right-hand page in their notebooks.

1. Add a Table of Contents entry for the Adjectives pages.

2. Cut out the title and glue it to the top of the page.

3. Cut out the definition piece and glue it below the title. Complete the definition of an adjective. (An adjective is a word that describes a **noun**. An adjective can describe color, size, shape, or how many.)

4. Cut out the flap book. Cut on the solid lines to create two flaps on each side. Apply glue to the back of the center section and attach it to the page.

5. Write adjectives that describe each object under the flaps.

Reflect on Learning

To complete the left-hand page, have students draw a picture of their favorite toys in the center of the page. Have students list adjectives that describe the toy around the picture. Allow time for students to share their work.

Adjectives

An **adjective** is a word that describes a
_____. An adjective can describe
color, size, shape, or how many.

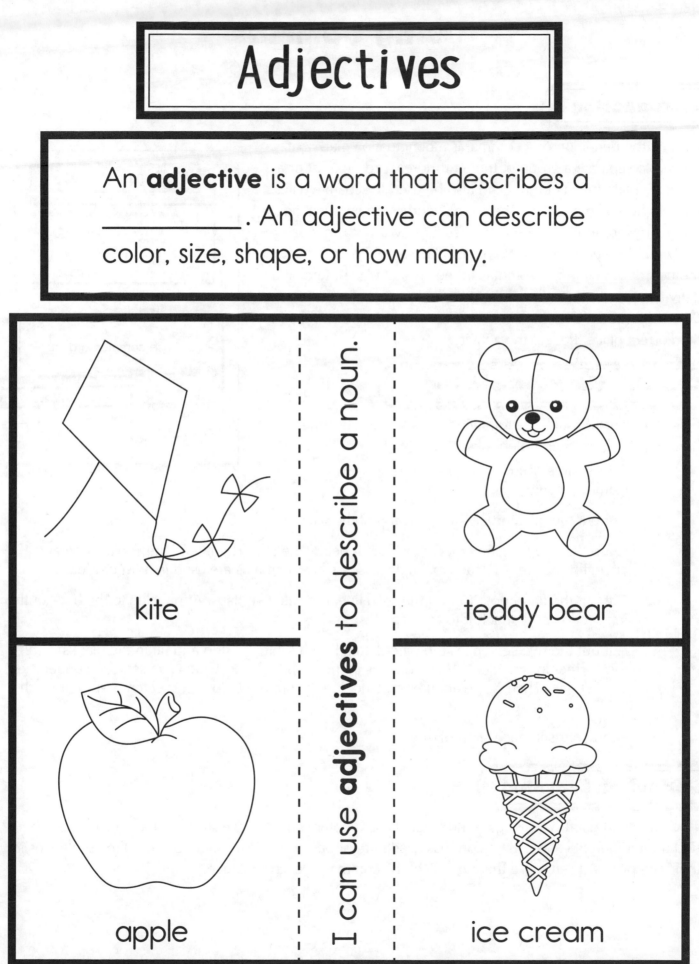

kite

teddy bear

apple

ice cream

I can use **adjectives** to describe a noun.

Using Commas

Introduction

Discuss the definition of a comma as a punctuation mark that is used to separate a group of three or more words in a list or a series. Explain that a comma can also be used to separate dates. Discuss how commas are used so that words and numbers do not get mixed up. Write a sentence such as *Mia can run, hop, and jump* but leave out the commas. Have a volunteer come to the board and write the commas in the correct places. Repeat the activity a few more times. Then, write a date such as *January 1, 2014* without the comma. Have a volunteer write the comma in the correct place. Repeat the activity.

Creating the Notebook Page

Guide students through the following steps to complete the right-hand page in their notebooks.

1. Add a Table of Contents entry for the Using Commas pages.

2. Cut out the title and glue it to the top of the page.

3. Cut out the explanation piece and glue it below the title. Then, read the explanation and circle the commas in each example. Discuss how commas are used in a list or a date.

4. Cut out the flap book. Cut on the solid line to create two flaps. Apply glue to the back of the left section and attach it to the page.

5. Cut out the two sentence strip pieces. Read each sentence strip and fill in the blanks with the correct information. Write commas in the proper places. Glue each sentence under the correct flap. Then, write another sentence using commas below the sentence strip or on the back of each flap.

6. Read your sentences to a partner.

Reflect on Learning

To complete the left-hand page, send students on a comma hunt. Have students look through books to find three different examples of commas used in a list or a date. Have students record the sentences in their notebooks. Then, have them highlight the commas in each sentence.

Using Commas

Use commas to separate a list of words in a sentence:

> I like to eat popcorn, ice cream, and cotton candy at the fair.

Use commas to separate the numbers in a date:

> I went to the fair on July 10, 2014.

I like to eat _____ _____ and _____.

My birthday is _____.

Use commas in a list.

Use commas in a date.

Synonyms

Introduction

Explain the definition of a synonym as a word that has a similar meaning to another word. Review several pairs of synonyms on the board. Next, play a matching game. Write synonyms on index cards. Create enough cards so that each student receives one. Distribute them to the class. Have students find other students who have matching synonyms. Redistribute the cards and repeat the activity.

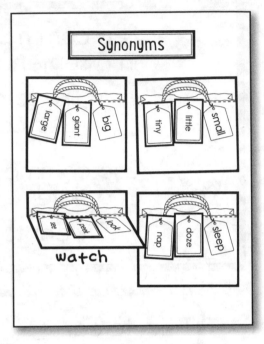

Creating the Notebook Page

Guide students through the following steps to complete the right-hand page in their notebooks.

1. Add a Table of Contents entry for the Synonyms pages.

2. Cut out the title and glue it to the top of the page.

3. Cut out the shopping bag flaps. Apply glue to the back of the top section of each flap and attach it to the page.

4. Cut out the word cards. Read each one and match the synonym to the correct bag. Then, glue the word onto the bag.

5. Write at least one more synonym for the words on the bag under each flap. Read your words to a partner.

Reflect on Learning

To complete the left-hand page, have students draw three shopping bags. Label the shopping bags with three verbs such as *said*, *laugh*, and *cry*. Have students brainstorm and write synonyms for each word on the bags. Allow time for students to share their work.

Synonyms

big

small

look

sleep

| doze | see | peek | giant |
| large | nap | tiny | little |

Pronouns

Introduction

Discuss the definition of a pronoun as a word that takes the place of one or more nouns. Discuss that the pronoun does not change who or what is being discussed. Call attention to how students refer to themselves when they are talking. They use words like *I*, *me*, and *my* instead of their own names. Review the pronouns *she*, *he*, *her*, *his*, *they*, *we*, *us*, and *them*.

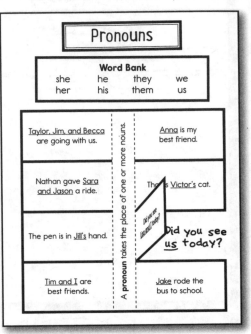

Creating the Notebook Page

Guide students through the following steps to complete the right-hand page in their notebooks.

1. Add a Table of Contents entry for the Pronouns pages.

2. Cut out the title and glue it to the top of the page.

3. Cut out the word bank and glue it below the title.

4. Cut out the flap book. Cut on the solid lines to create four flaps on each side. Apply glue to the back of the center section and attach it to the page.

5. Read each sentence. Replace the noun(s) in the sentence with a pronoun from the word bank. Rewrite each sentence with the correct pronoun under the flaps. Underline the pronoun in each sentence.

Reflect on Learning

To complete the left-hand page, have students number their pages from 1 to 10. Read 10 sentences aloud with a noun or nouns that could be replaced with pronouns. Have students decide which pronoun should replace the noun or nouns in each sentence and write them next to the correct number.

Pronouns

Taylor, Jim, and Becca are going with us.

Anna is my best friend.

Nathan gave Sara and Jason a ride.

That is Victor's cat.

The pen is in Jill's hand.

Did you see Lisa and I today?

Tim and I are best friends.

Jake rode the bus to school.

A pronoun takes the place of one or more nouns.

Word Bank

she	he	they	we
her	his	them	us

Asking and Answering Questions

Introduction

Explain how asking and answering questions about a text helps readers to better understand the text. Discuss using the five Ws (*who, what, when, where,* and *why*) and how to ask questions before, during, and after reading. Choose a picture book or informational text to read to the class. Model asking and answering questions about the text before, during, and after the reading.

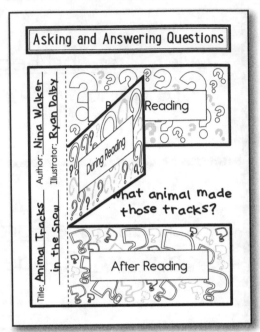

Creating the Notebook Page

Guide students through the following steps to complete the right-hand page in their notebooks.

1. Add a Table of Contents entry for the Asking and Answering Questions pages.

2. Cut out the title and glue it to the top of the page.

3. Cut out the flap book. Cut on the solid lines to create three flaps. Apply glue to the back of the left section and attach it to the page.

4. Choose a book to read. Before reading, preview the book and write any questions you may have about the book. Write them under the *Before Reading* flap. During reading, write any questions you may have about the book under the *During Reading* flap. When you are finished reading, write any questions you may still have under the *After Reading* flap.

5. As you come across the answers to your questions while reading, write them under the appropriate flaps.

Reflect on Learning

To complete the left-hand page, have students trace around their hands. Have them write one of the 5 Ws in each of the fingers and *how* in the middle of the palm. Use this page as a reference tool.

Asking and Answering Questions

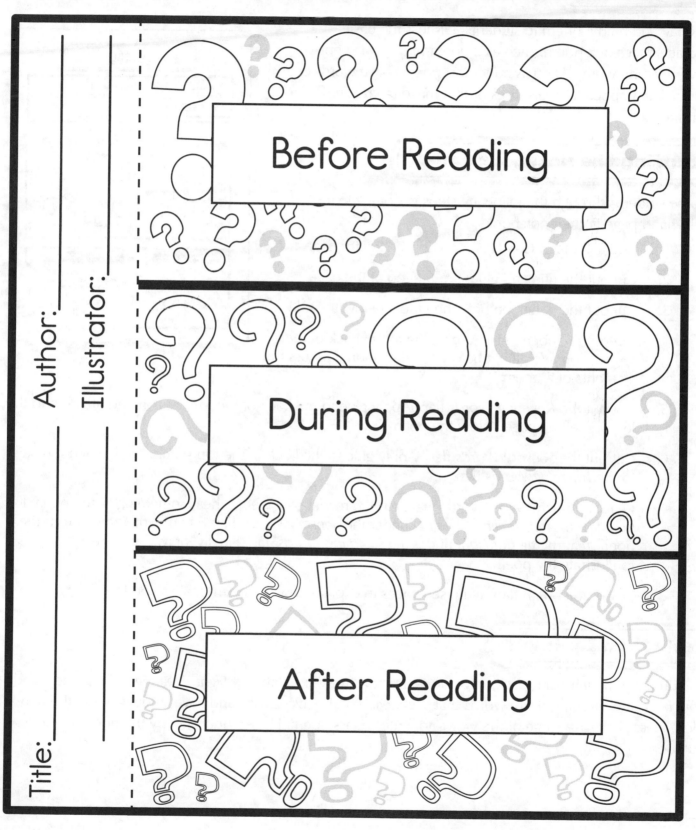

Author:

Illustrator:

Title:

Before Reading

During Reading

After Reading

Poetry

Introduction

Display and read a poem to students. Discuss the basic characteristics of a poem, such as a poem may or may not have rhyming words. Discuss how most poems have words or phrases that appeal to the senses or that make the reader feel a certain way.

Creating the Notebook Page

Guide students through the following steps to complete the right-hand page in their notebooks.

1. Add a Table of Contents entry for the Poetry pages.

2. Cut out the title and glue it to the top of the page.

3. Cut out the definition box and glue it below the title.

4. Cut out the poem flap. Apply glue to the back of the top section and glue it below the definition. Discuss the elements of a poem.

5. Cut out the *Rhyming Words* flap. Apply glue to the back of the top section and attach it to the left side of the page below the poem.

6. Cut out the *Sensory Words* flap. Apply glue to the back of the top section and attach it next to the *Rhyming Words* flap.

7. Read the poem. Write words that help the reader see, feel, or hear something in the poem (*roll, laughs, fun, smiling, tinkling*) under the *Sensory Words* flap. Then, write words from the poem that rhyme (*fun/sun*) under the *Rhyming Words* flap. Finally, draw a picture to illustrate the poem.

8. Under the poem flap, write sentences to explain how the poem makes you feel.

Reflect on Learning

To complete the left-hand page, have students draw five boxes labeled *Sight, Hearing, Taste, Smell,* and *Touch*. As a class, brainstorm words that show each of the five senses and have students write them in the boxes. Then, use some of the words to write a class poem. Have students copy the poem in their notebooks.

Poetry

A **poem** is a collection of words that expresses an idea or makes you feel a certain way. A poem has rhythm. A poem can have words that rhyme.

My Baby Brother

My baby brother rides in his stroller
While I'm on my bike.
We roll down the sidewalk in the sun.
My brother laughs at me riding.
He thinks it's fun
To see his sister smiling
And hear my bell tinkling
And feel my streamers flapping
   in his face.

Rhyming
Words

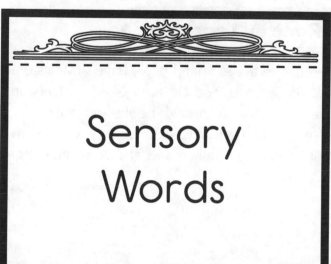

Sensory
Words

Text Features

Introduction

Display a nonfiction book. Explain the definition of text features as parts of a nonfiction book that help readers know where to look to find information. Discuss and show how the title page tells the title, author, and illustrator of the book. Explain how the table of contents lets the reader know where to find a topic or chapter and on what page it can be found. Discuss how some informational books have a glossary, usually at the end of a book, to give the reader definitions and pronunciations of difficult words that are used in the book. Explain how some fictional books can also have a title page and a table of contents.

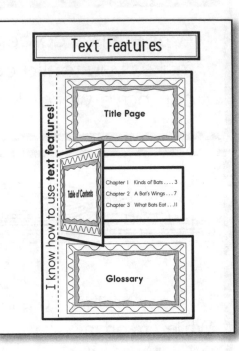

Creating the Notebook Page

Guide students through the following steps to complete the right-hand page in their notebooks.

1. Add a Table of Contents entry for the Text Features pages.

2. Cut out the title and glue it to the top of the page.

3. Cut out the flap book. Cut on the solid lines to create three flaps. Apply glue to the back of the left section and attach it to the page.

4. Cut out the text feature example cards. Read each card and decide which text feature it represents. Then, glue it under the correct flap.

5. On the back of each flap, write what each text feature is used for. For example, for the glossary flap, write *helps to find the meaning of hard words*.

Reflect on Learning

To complete the left-hand page, have students draw lines to make three columns labeled *Title Page, Table of Contents,* and *Glossary*. Send students on a text feature hunt using books in the classroom. Have students look through books and make tally marks under each column when they find a particular text feature in a book. Have them look through as many books as possible in the allotted time. Students should count their tally marks and compare their results with a partner.

Text Features

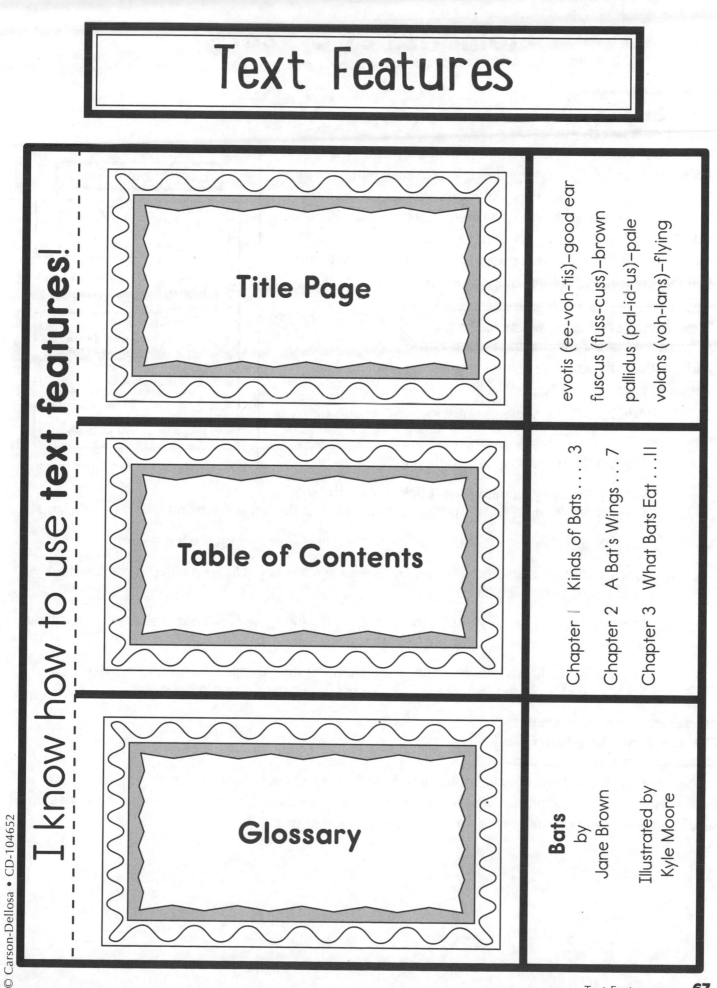

I know how to use **text features!**

Title Page

evotis (ee-voh-tis)–good ear

fuscus (fuss-cuss)–brown

pallidus (pal-id-us)–pale

volans (voh-lans)–flying

Table of Contents

Chapter 1   Kinds of Bats 3

Chapter 2   A Bat's Wings . . . 7

Chapter 3   What Bats Eat . . . 11

Glossary

Bats
by
Jane Brown

Illustrated by
Kyle Moore

Elements of a Story

Introduction

Draw three boxes on the board. Label the boxes *Characters*, *Setting*, and *Events*. Discuss the definitions of each part of a story. Then, read a short fiction book. After reading, discuss each of the elements of the book and write them in the squares. Remind students that the events of a story have to occur in the correct sequence to make sense. Pair students together and have them retell the story to each other using the information on the board.

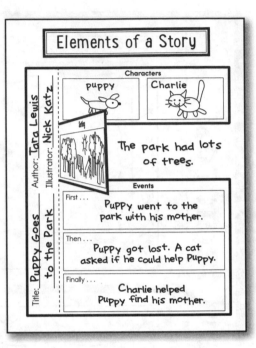

Creating the Notebook Page

Guide students through the following steps to complete the right-hand page in their notebooks.

1. Add a Table of Contents entry for the Elements of a Story pages.

2. Cut out the title and glue it to the top of the page.

3. Cut out the story elements flap book. Cut on the solid lines to create three flaps. Apply glue to the back of the left section and attach it to the page.

4. Read or listen to a story. Write the title, author, and illustrator on the left section.

5. Draw two characters from the story on the *Characters* flap. Under the flap, write a sentence about your favorite character.

6. Draw the setting of the story on the *Settings* flap. Under the flap, write a sentence describing the setting.

7. On the *Events* flap, write the main events from the story using the words, *First, Then,* and *Finally*. Under the flap, draw a picture of your favorite event in the story.

Reflect on Learning

To complete the left-hand page, have students draw three large circles labeled *Characters*, *Setting*, and *Events*. Have students plan short stories using their graphic organizers. Have them write their stories on a separate sheet of paper. Allow time for students to share their work.

68

Elements of a Story

Characters

Setting

Events

First . . .

Then . . .

Finally . . .

Author:

Illustrator:

Title:

Main Topic and Details

Introduction

Explain that a topic is the main idea of a text and that details give more information about the topic. Say words such as *sandwich*, *fruit*, and *juice*. Ask students what the topic might be for these words. A possible answer might be *lunch*. Write a topic on the board such as *school*. Have students provide details for the topic. Possible answers may include *desks*, *classroom*, and *backpacks*. List the details as students provide them. Repeat this activity a few more times with different topics.

Creating the Notebook Page

Guide students through the following steps to complete the right-hand page in their notebooks.

1. Add a Table of Contents entry for the Main Topic and Details pages.

2. Cut out the title and glue it to the top of the page.

3. Cut out the flap book. Cut on the solid lines to create two flaps. Apply glue to the back of the top section and attach it below the title.

4. Cut out the picture cards. Look at each picture and decide which topic it represents. Glue the picture cards under the correct flaps.

5. On the blank cards, draw an additional detail for each topic. Glue the cards under the correct flap.

6. Write the definition of the words *main topic* and *details* below the flaps. (The main topic is what the subject is about. The details tell more about the main topic.)

Reflect on Learning

To complete the left-hand page, have students draw a crayon box labeled with a main idea such as *Football* or *Dance*. Then, have students draw three large crayons around the box. Have them think of three details that support the main idea, and then write or draw the details on each of the crayons.

Context Clues

Introduction

Explain the definition of context clues as hints or clues in a sentence or paragraph that help the reader understand an unknown word in a text. Discuss how context clues can be found in words, pictures, or definitions. Model how to read around an unknown word to find its meaning.

Creating the Notebook Page

Guide students through the following steps to complete the right-hand page in their notebooks.

1. Add a Table of Contents entry for the Context Clues pages.

2. Cut out the title and glue it to the top of the page.

3. Cut out the word bank. Glue it below the title.

4. Cut out the context clues piece and glue it to the page.

5. Read each sentence about the butterfly life cycle. Use context clues to decide which word from the word bank should be written in the blank to make the sentence correct. Cross the words off as you use them. (All of the words in the word bank will not be used.)

Reflect on Learning

To complete the left-hand page, write two sentences containing a nonsense word on the board. For example, *Butterflies **krick** nectar with their tongues*. Have students read the sentences. Then, students should use context clues to rewrite the sentences replacing the nonsense words with the correct words.

Context Clues

I know how to use **context clues**!

The butterfly lays one _____ on a milkweed leaf. It will soon hatch.

The egg hatches into a small fuzzy _____. He is hungry and looks for food.

The hungry caterpillar eats the _____ on a tree.

The caterpillar grows, and after two or three weeks, is ready to _____.

He can form a _____ or brown chrysalis.

The caterpillar is now a beautiful _____.

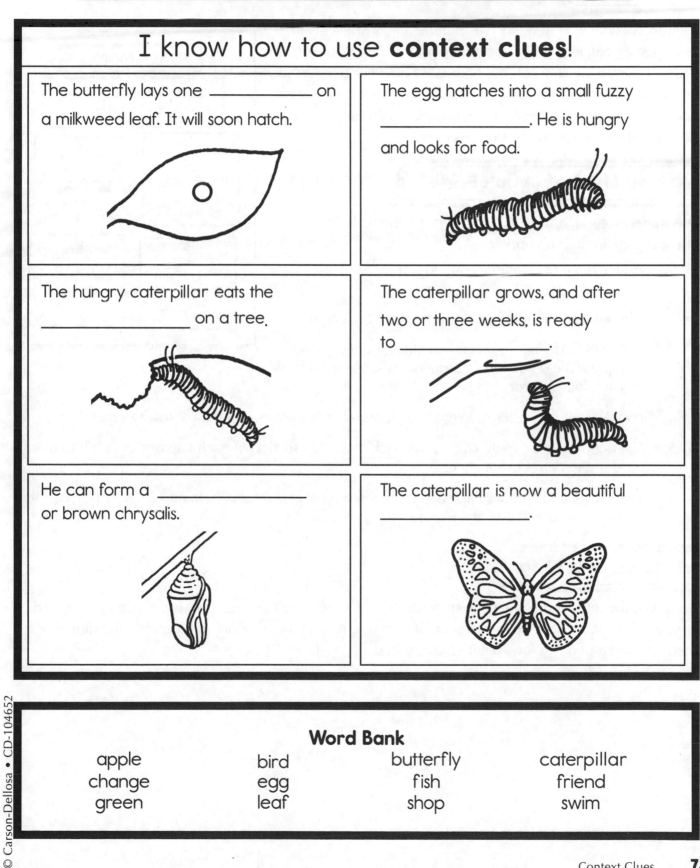

Word Bank

apple	bird	butterfly	caterpillar
change	egg	fish	friend
green	leaf	shop	swim

Sequencing

Introduction

Explain the definition of sequence as putting things or events in order. Have a volunteer describe how he gets ready for school. As he explains, write the steps on the board. Number the steps as you write them. Discuss how events in books follow a sequence from the beginning to the end. Explain that a story would be difficult to understand if the events in the story were not in order.

Creating the Notebook Page

Guide students through the following steps to complete the right-hand page in their notebooks.

1. Add a Table of Contents entry for the Sequencing pages.

2. Cut out the title and glue it to the top of the page.

3. Cut out the definition piece and glue it below the title. Complete the definition of sequence. (Sequence means to put things in **order**.)

4. Look at the picture flaps. Write *1, 2, 3,* and *4* in the boxes to put the cards in order.

5. Cut out the flaps. Apply glue to the back of the top section of each flap and attach it to the page in the correct sequence.

6. Write a sentence under each flap using the words, *First, Next, Then,* and *Finally* to explain the steps involved in drawing a picture.

Reflect on Learning

To complete the left-hand page, have students draw and number the steps they go through to get ready for bed each night. Allow students to share their work. As a class, compare and contrast the different sequences that students follow to get ready for bed.

Sequencing

Sequence means to put things in _____.

CD-104652

Fiction and Nonfiction

Introduction

Display a variety of fiction and nonfiction books. Ask students to compare the books. Possible answers may include that they all have front and back covers, that some of the books have real pictures, and that some of the books have characters in them. Display a fiction book and explain that fiction is a story that is not real. It is a make-believe story. Display a nonfiction book and discuss how it contains real facts and pictures. Read a few book titles aloud and have the students guess if each book is fiction or nonfiction based on the title.

Creating the Notebook Page

Guide students through the following steps to complete the right-hand page in their notebooks.

1. Add a Table of Contents entry for the Fiction and Nonfiction pages.

2. Cut out the title and glue it to the top of the page.

3. Cut out the *Fiction* flap. Apply glue to the back of the top section and attach it below the title.

4. Cut out the *Nonfiction* flap. Apply glue to the back of the top section and attach it to the bottom of the page.

5. Cut out the picture cards. Look at each book cover and decide if the cover would be for a fiction or nonfiction book. Glue the book covers on the correct flaps.

6. Write two titles of fiction books you have read under the fiction flap.

7. Write two titles of nonfiction books you have read under the nonfiction flap.

Reflect on Learning

To complete the left-hand page, have students draw book covers for a nonfiction book. Then, have them draw book covers for a fiction book. Allow time for students to share their work and explain their book covers.

Fiction is a story that is not real.

Nonfiction is a text about real things.

Tabs

Cut out each tab and label it. Apply glue to the back of each tab and align it on the outside edge of the page with only the label section showing beyond the edge. Then, fold each tab to seal the page inside.

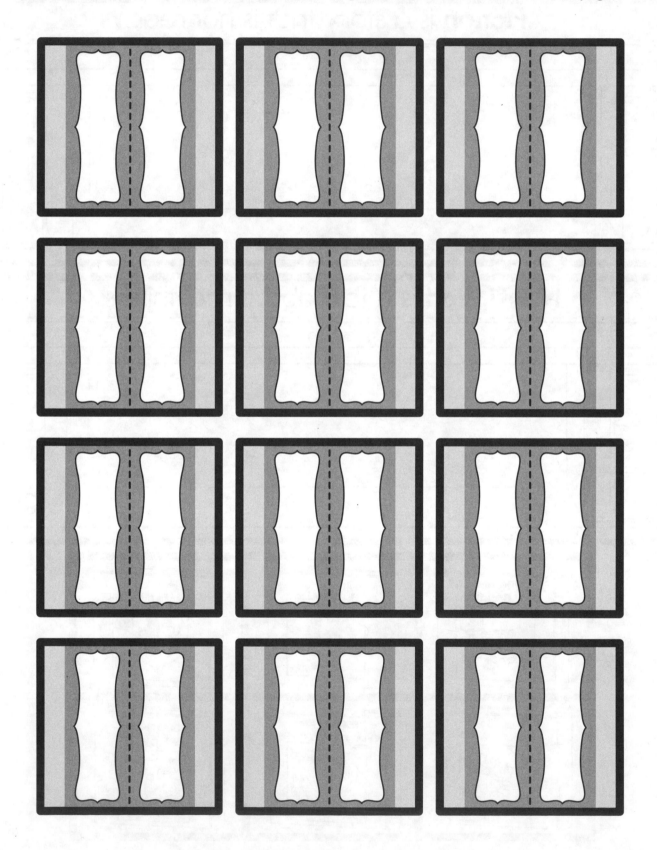

Cut out the KWL chart and cut on the solid lines to create three separate flaps. Apply glue to the back of the Topic section to attach the chart to a notebook page.

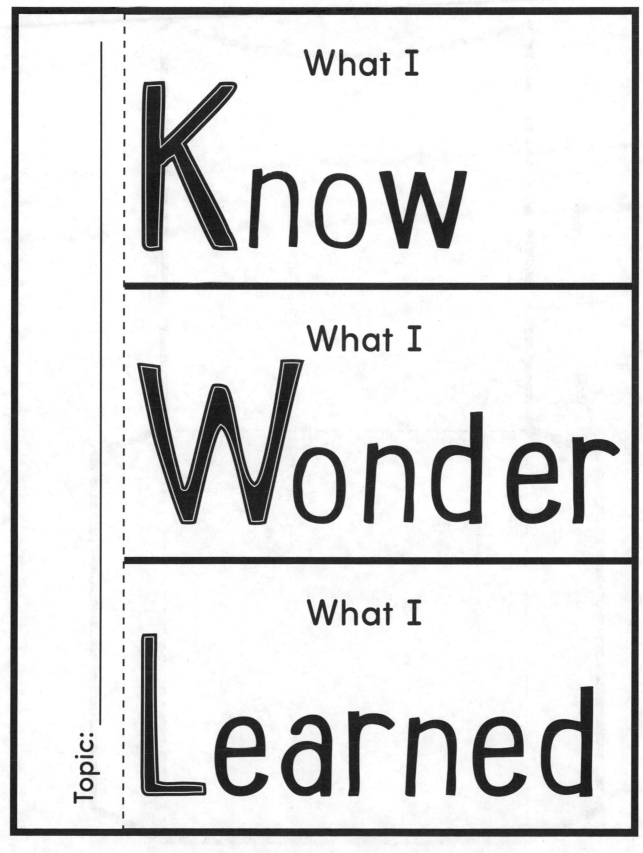

What I

Know

What I

Wonder

What I

Learned

Topic: _____

Library Pocket

Cut out the library pocket on the solid lines. Fold in the side tabs and apply glue to them before folding up the front of the pocket. Apply glue to the back of the pocket to attach it to a notebook page.

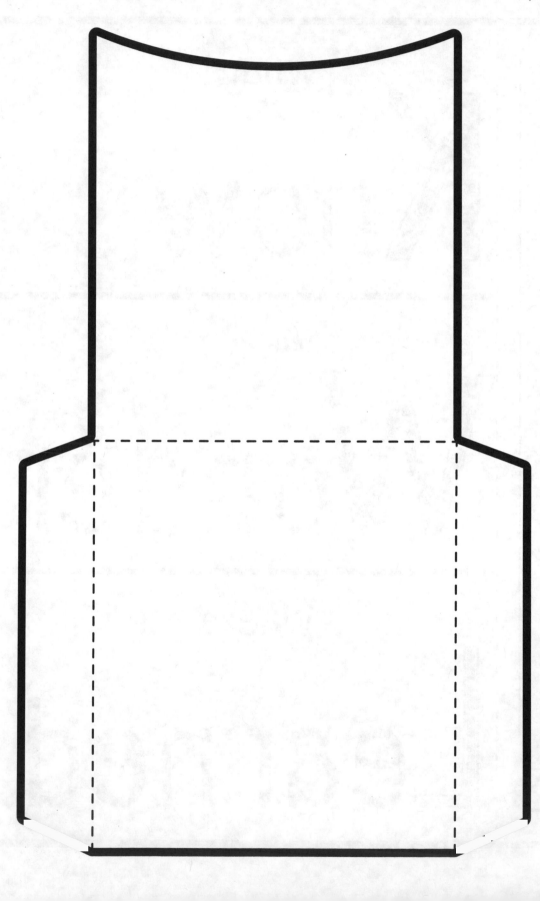

80

Cut out the envelope on the solid lines. Fold in the side tabs and apply glue to them before folding up the rectangular front of the envelope. Fold down the triangular flap to close the envelope. Apply glue to the back of the envelope to attach it to a notebook page.

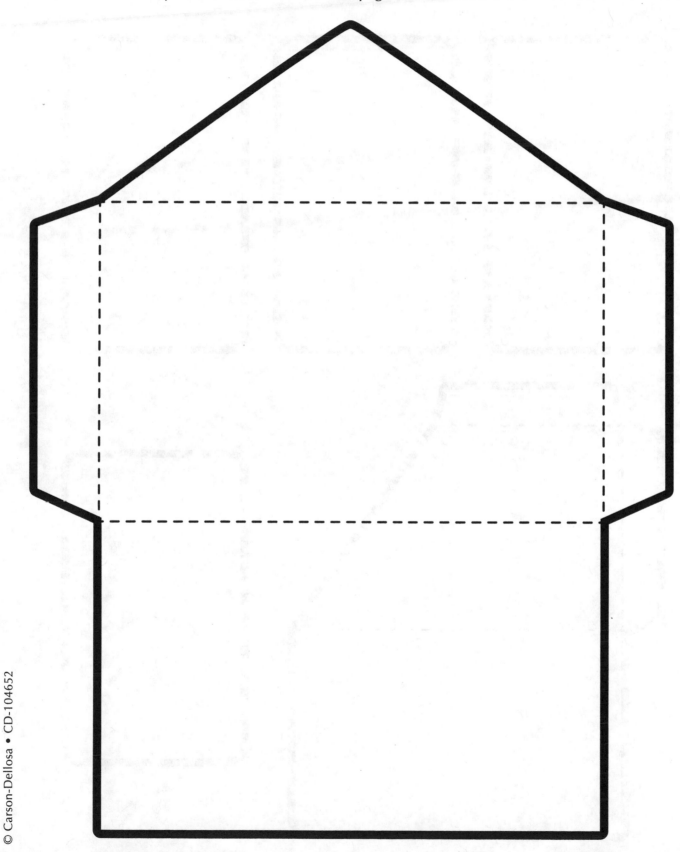

Cut out the pocket on the solid lines. Fold over the front of the pocket. Then, apply glue to the tabs and fold them around the back of the pocket. Apply glue to the back of the pocket to attach it to a notebook page. Cut out the cards and store them in the envelope.

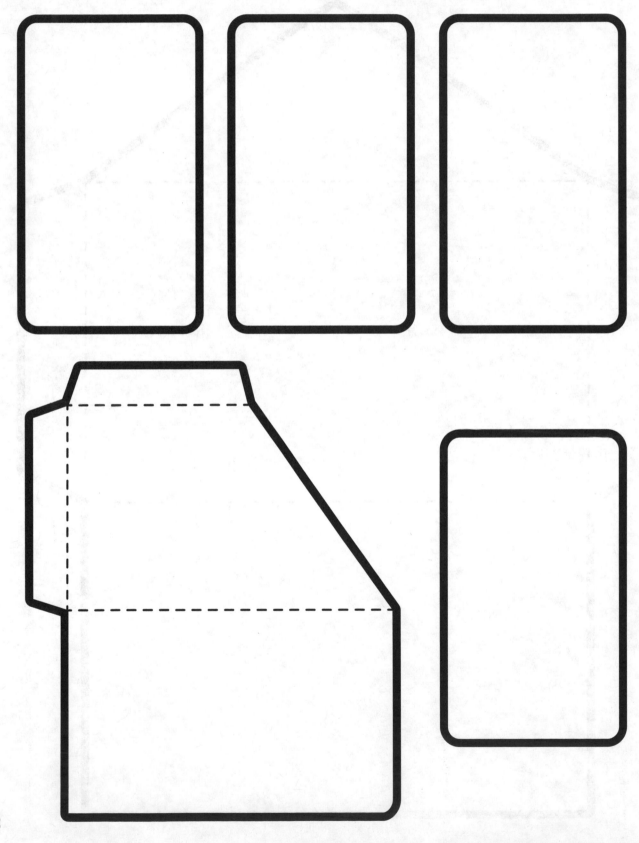

Six-Flap Shutter Fold

Cut out the shutter fold around the outside border. Then, cut on the solid lines to create six flaps. Fold the flaps toward the center. Apply glue to the back of the shutter fold to attach it to a notebook page.

If desired, this template can be modified to create a four-flap shutter fold by cutting off the bottom row. You can also create two three-flap books by cutting it in half down the center line.

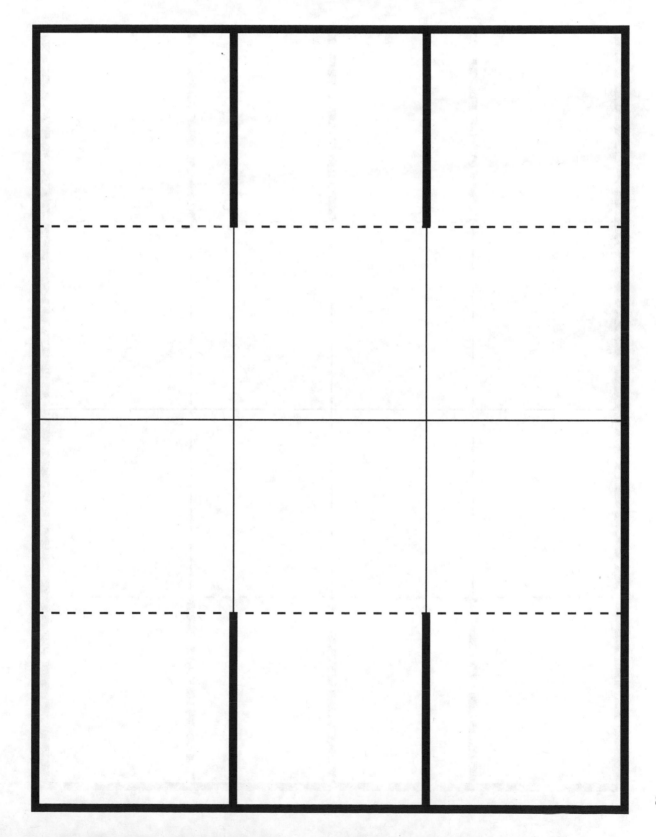

Eight-Flap Shutter Fold

Cut out the shutter fold around the outside border. Then, cut on the solid lines to create eight flaps. Fold the flaps toward the center. Apply glue to the back of the shutter fold to attach it to a notebook page.

If desired, this template can be modified to create two four-flap shutter folds by cutting off the bottom two rows. You can also create two four-flap books by cutting it in half down the center line.

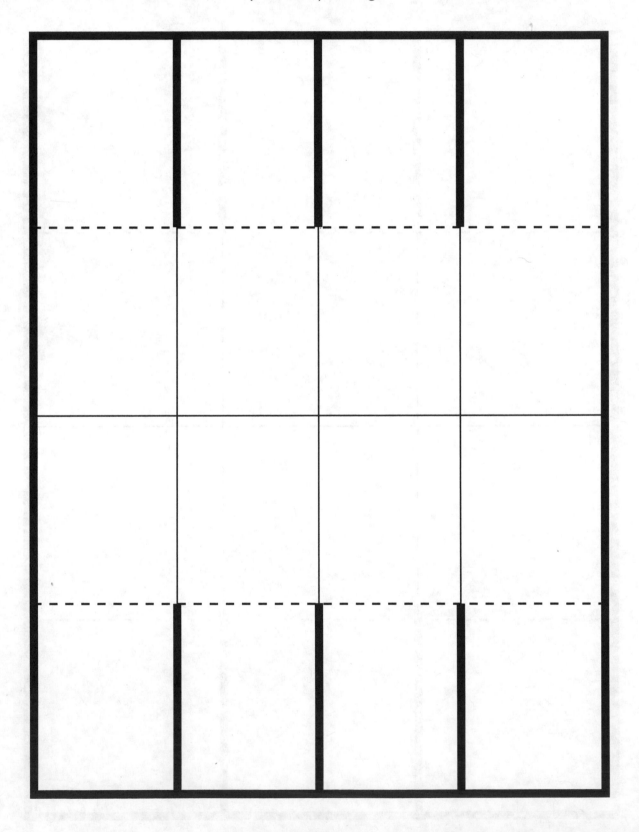

Flap Book—Eight Flaps

Cut out the flap book around the outside border. Then, cut on the solid lines to create eight flaps. Apply glue to the back of the center section to attach it to a notebook page.

If desired, this template can be modified to create a six-flap or two four-flap books by cutting off the bottom row or two. You can also create a tall four-flap book by cutting off the flaps on the left side.

Flap Book—Twelve Flaps

Cut out the flap book around the outside border. Then, cut on the solid lines to create 12 flaps. Apply glue to the back of the center section to attach it to a notebook page.

If desired, this template can be modified to create smaller flap books by cutting off any number of rows from the bottom. You can also create a tall flap book by cutting off the flaps on the left side.

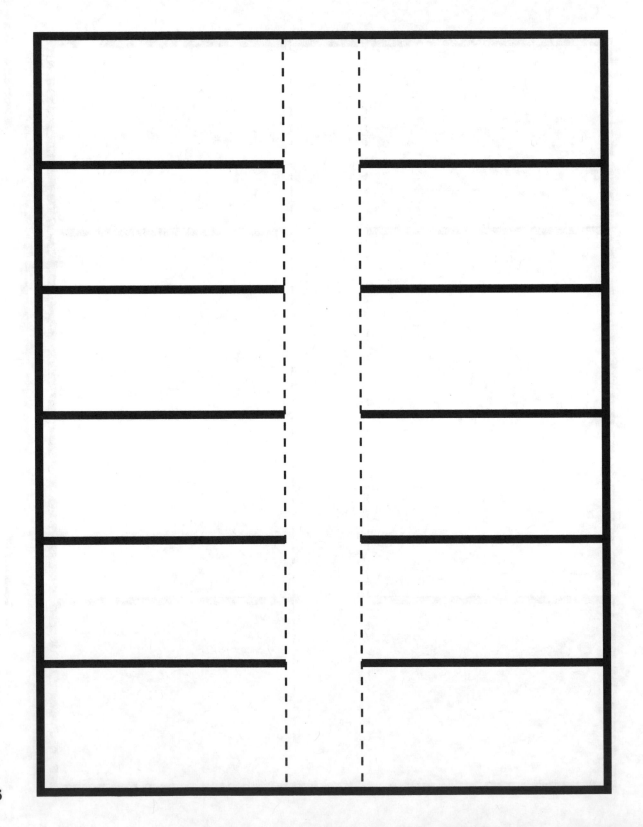

Shaped Flaps

Cut out each shaped flap. Apply glue to the back of the narrow section to attach it to a notebook page.

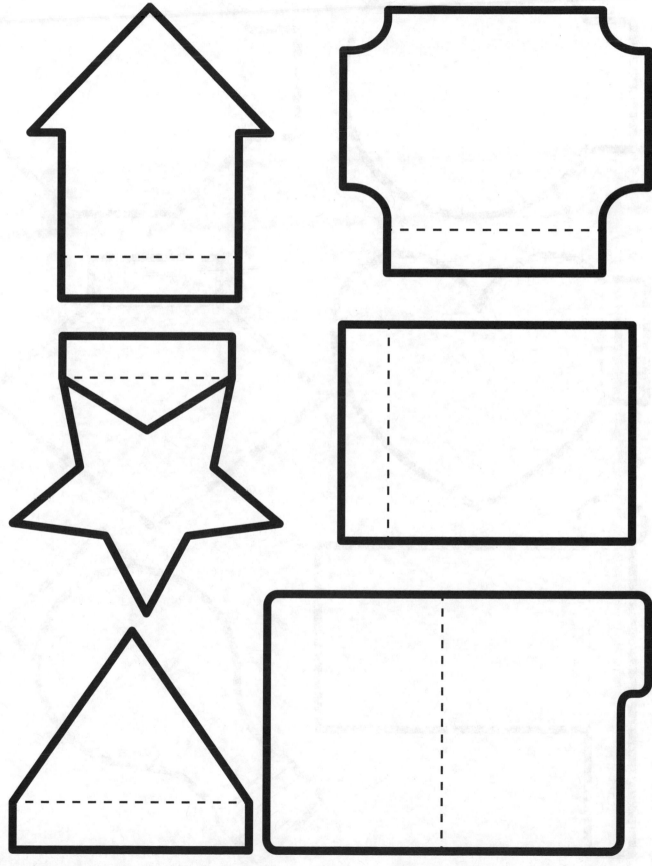

Shaped Flaps

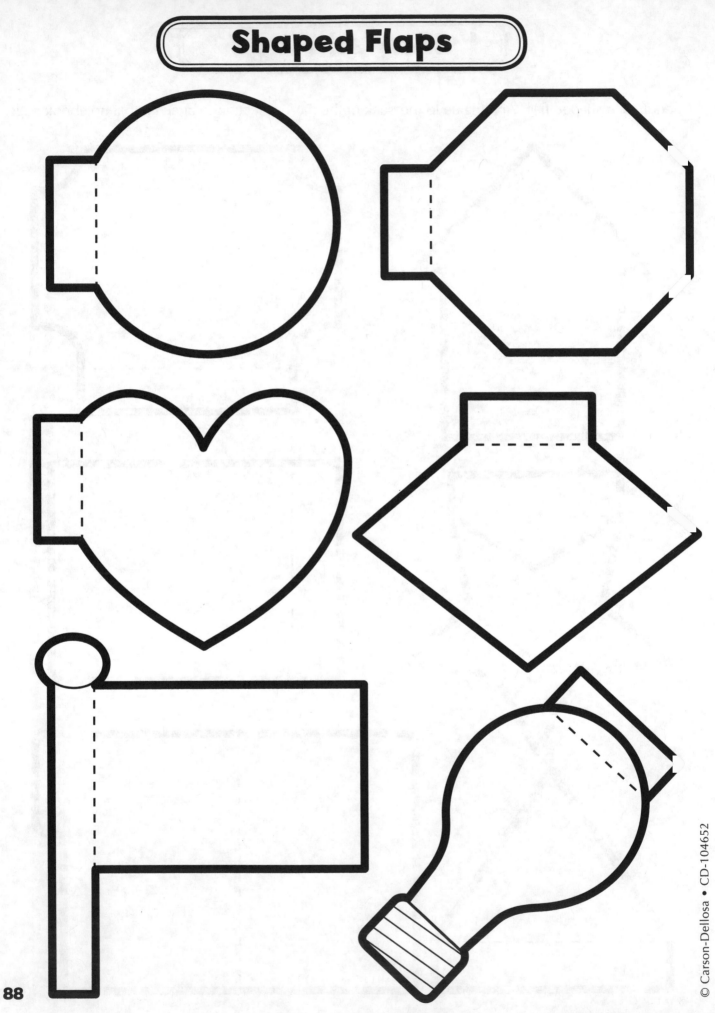

Interlocking Booklet

Cut out the booklet on the solid lines, including the short vertical lines on the top and bottom flaps. Then, fold the top and bottom flaps toward the center, interlocking them using the small vertical cuts. Apply glue to the back of the center panel to attach it to a notebook page.

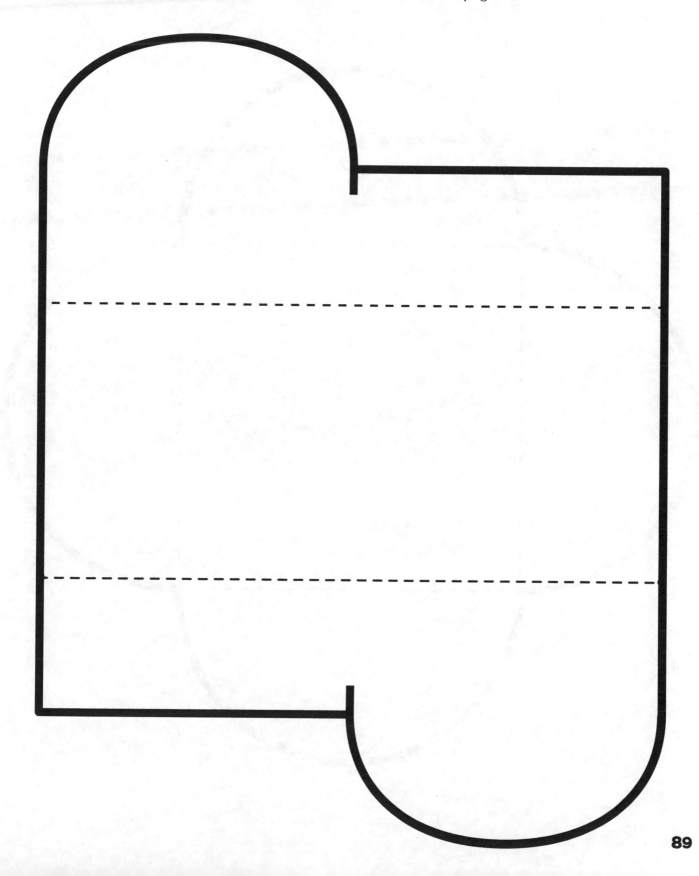

Cut out the shape on the solid lines. Then, fold the flaps toward the center. Apply glue to the back of the center panel to attach it to a notebook page.

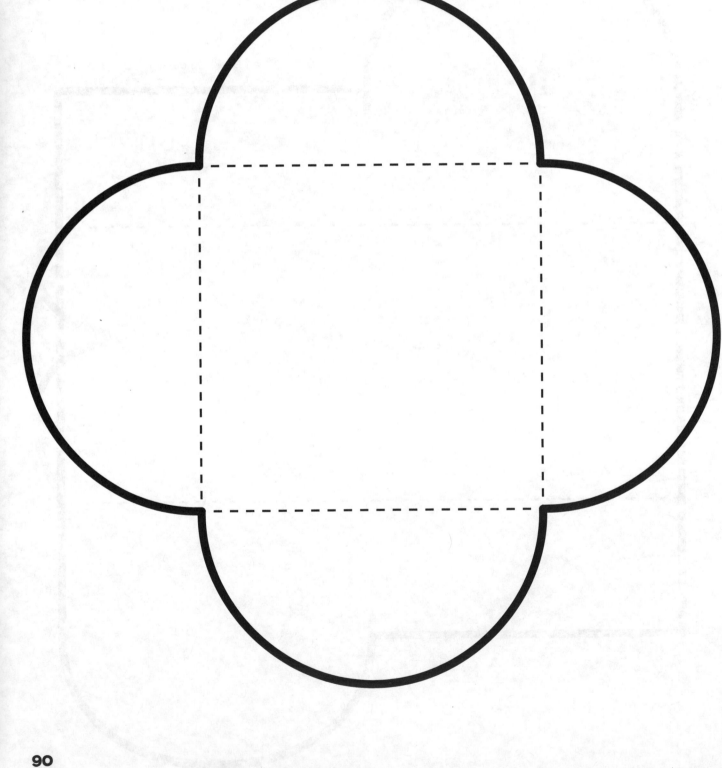

Six-Flap Petal Fold

Cut out the shape on the solid lines. Then, fold the flaps toward the center and back out. Apply glue to the back of the center panel to attach it to a notebook page.

Accordion Folds

Cut out the accordion pieces on the solid lines. Fold on the dashed lines, alternating the fold direction. Apply glue to the back of the last section to attach it to a notebook page.

You may modify the accordion books to have more or fewer pages by cutting off extra pages or by having students glue the first and last panels of two accordion books together.

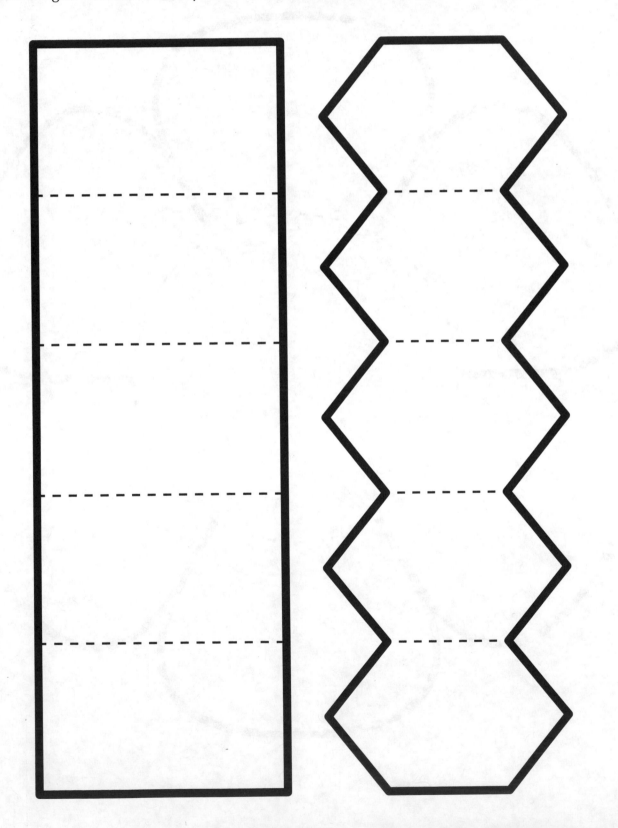

Accordion Folds

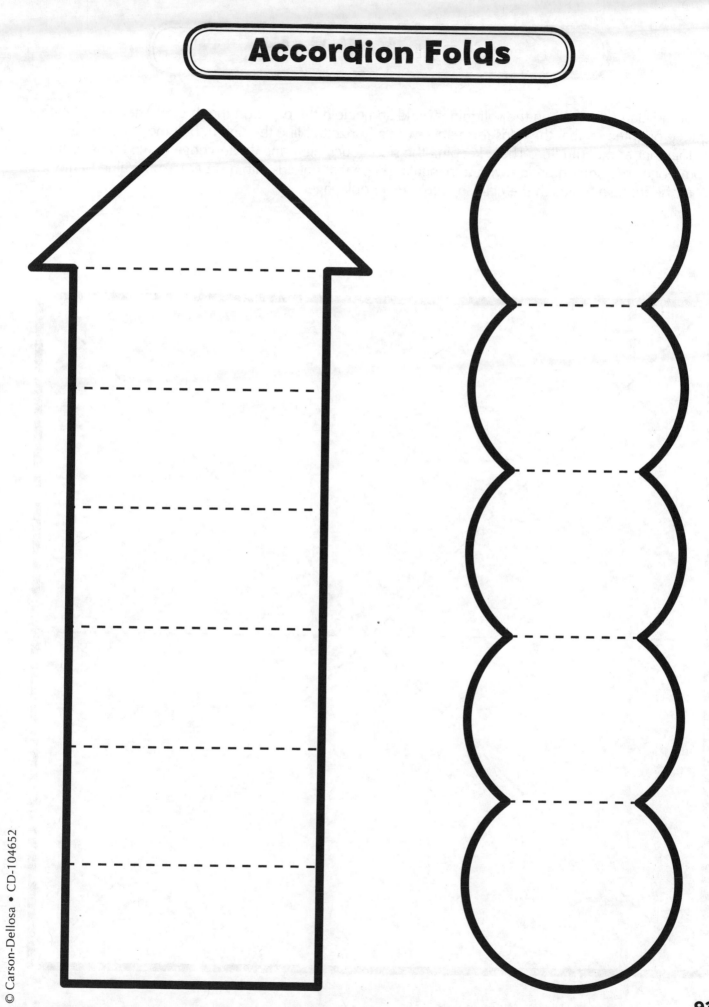

Clamshell Fold

Cut out the clamshell fold on the solid lines. Fold and unfold the piece on the three dashed lines. With the piece oriented so that the folds form an X with a horizontal line through it, pull the left and right sides together at the fold line. Then, keeping the sides touching, bring the top edge down to meet the bottom edge. You should be left with a triangular shape that unfolds into a square. Apply glue to the back of the triangle to attach the clamshell to a notebook page.

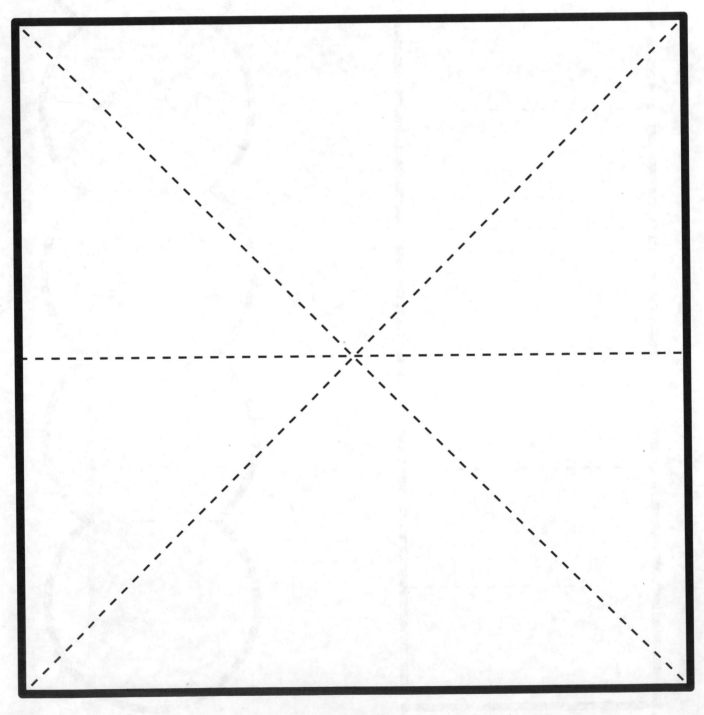

Puzzle Pieces

Cut out each puzzle along the solid lines to create a three- or four-piece puzzle. Apply glue to the back of each puzzle piece to attach it to a notebook page. Alternately, apply glue only to one edge of each piece to create flaps.

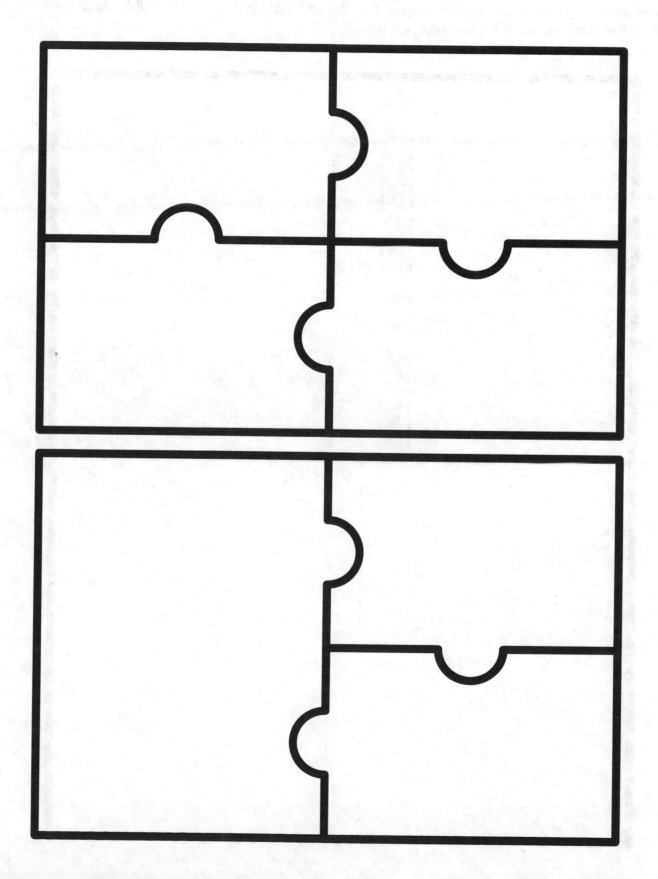

Flip Book

Cut out the two rectangular pieces on the solid lines. Fold each rectangle on the dashed lines. Fold the first piece so the gray glue section is inside the fold. Apply glue to the gray glue section and place the other folded rectangle on top so that the folds are nested and create a book with four cascading flaps. Make sure that the inside pages are facing up so that the edges of both pages are visible. Apply glue to the back of the book to attach it to a notebook page.

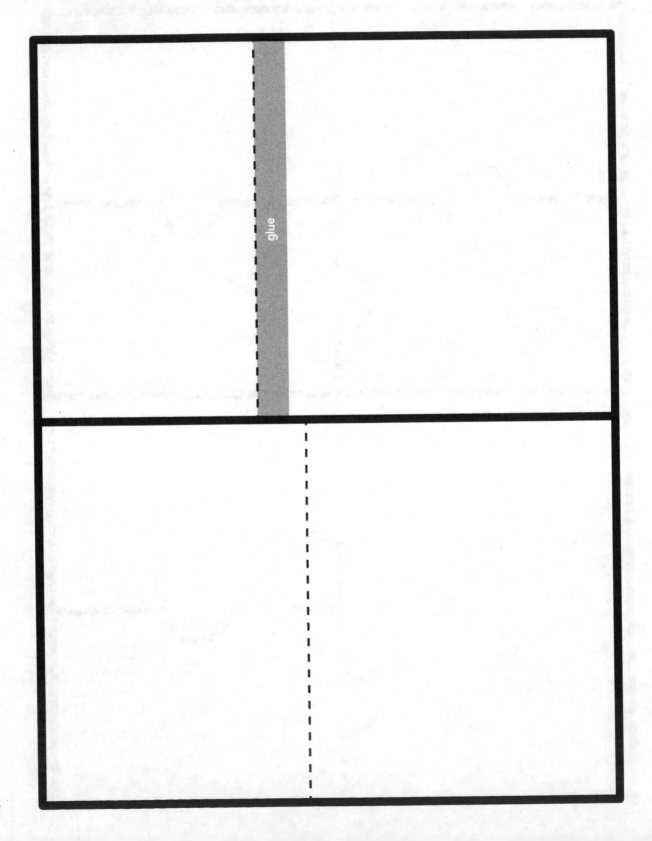

© Carson-Dellosa • CD-104652